03 WRITE ON TARGET **INTRODUCTION:**
OUR AIMS

'Write on Target' builds on from the previous publications, 'Raising Standards in Writing' (2002), and 'Strategies for Immediate Impact on Writing Standards' (2003).

Both the previous publications address a new teaching methodology for raising standards in writing rapidly and effectively. The method is based on fast, fun and lively teaching of the 'writing voice' through oracy. It gives pupils confidence and the understanding to develop control of a higher level writing voice without requiring the understanding of technical knowledge of syntax and grammatical analysis. This is important as not all primary aged children are ready for the level of technical knowledge and understanding required to access higher order language in this way.

'Raising Standards in Writing' (2002) explains how the methodology developed and examines issues around assessment, tracking, monitoring and target setting within a long term strategy to raise standards in writing. It then introduces the philosophy and approach of quick impact teaching.

'Strategies for Immediate Impact on Writing Standards' (2003) provides a synopsis of all the content of the previous book, and then develops and extends the teaching strategies. It provides evidence of significantly raised standards within very short time scales, PLUS the lesson plans and resources used by a large number of Year 6 teachers to raise standards beyond those expected between January and May of the year of testing.

'Write on Target' (2005) aims to:

- provide an overview of the long term strategy and the quick impact methods for teaching (this may be by-passed by those already confidently teaching through 'Big Writing' or used as a self evaluation tool to verify that all the recommended elements are in place);

- advise and support the target setting process;

- provide a definition of, and model for, use of Assessment for Learning in all subjects in all classrooms;

- examine issues around the underachievement of many boys and some girls in writing;

- provide two models for quick intervention;

- provide further evidence and case studies;

- provide further teaching activities;

- provide a draft Criterion Scale model for use within the Scottish levels for writing.

Sincere thanks are given to the many teachers who have provided materials, case studies and other evidence of success to further inform this initiative.

Use the following as check lists to ensure you are addressing all elements. If in doubt read the two previous publications, a synopsis of which is provided in Chapter 1.

STRATEGIES FOR QUICK IMPACT:

- [ ] The importance of speaking and listening skills
- [ ] The importance of ethos and the teaching environment
- [ ] The importance of self esteem
- [ ] Teaching to the targets
- [ ] Warm ups and games
- [ ] Addressing all learning styles
- [ ] Celebration and scoring of goals
- [ ] Assessment for learning – KIDS IN THE LOOP!!!
- [ ] Tracking and monitoring
- [ ] Praise and feedback

CHANGES TO THE CLASSROOM:

- [ ] Soften the lights
- [ ] Large aroma candle burning
- [ ] Soft music (Mozart) playing
- [ ] Pupils' writing portfolios on the tables
- [ ] A4 (A5 in Year 1) lined paper with a margin on the tables
- [ ] Special pens on the tables
- [ ] 3 goals (fruit in the writing session) on the tables
- [ ] Silence for writing

OPPORTUNITIES FOR THE FOUR GENERIC TARGETS:

- [ ] Warm ups before literacy hours
- [ ] Last few minutes of lessons
- [ ] Shared reading and writing
- [ ] Text level work
- [ ] Extended writing in all subjects
- [ ] Reading text in all subjects

OTHER VCOP ASPECTS:

- [ ] Importance of environment
- [ ] Constant collection of vocabulary and activities for 'ownership'
- [ ] Use of connective fans
- [ ] Constant focus on the 3 power openers (connectives, 'ing' words and 'ly' words
- [ ] Punctuation / punctuation pyramid games
- [ ] Up-levelling
- [ ] Explicit teaching
- [ ] The display
- [ ] ORACY! ORACY! ORACY!

THE TEACHER'S ROLE DURING THE WRITING SESSION:

- ☐ Sit quietly and do not intrude
- ☐ Give the ten minute time prompts

THE ROLE OF THE TEACHER IN THE LONG TERM STRATEGY:

- ☐ Plan and manage the termly assessments (December, March, May) and the September 'Summer Dip' check.
- ☐ Use the Criterion Scale to assess and set targets.
- ☐ Manage the photocopying of every assessed piece.
- ☐ Send photocopies to the 'driver' of the initiative.
- ☐ Remove numerical judgement from the front of assessed original.
- ☐ Insert the assessed original in class portfolio.
- ☐ Update the tracker and calculate the Value Added (VA) in sub-levels.
- ☐ Copy the tracker and send to the 'driver' with the other copies.
- ☐ Insert the tracker in the front of the class portfolio.
- ☐ Send the class portfolio to the next teacher at the end of the year.

THE ROLE OF THE 'DRIVER' IN THE LONG TERM STRATEGY:

- ☐ Oversee the management of the school evidence base, including the insertion of the trackers and pupils' assessed writing within the class section of the uni-lever ring binder/s.
- ☐ Oversee the timing and implementation of the termly assessments, ensuring that all staff use the same text type and that the stimulus is appropriate and will engage all pupils.
- ☐ Monitor progress within classes and across cohorts through the updated trackers and through examining the evidence in pupils' pockets when appropriate.
- ☐ Praise teachers and pupils when progress is very good.
- ☐ Identify particularly successful teacher/s as peer coaches.
- ☐ Discuss any pupils making little or no progress with the teacher, and once a term or year with all teachers in a meeting.
- ☐ Calculate/adjust whole school targets based on teachers' May assessments and targets. Set challenging aspirational targets for internal use. Inform all parties when targets have been adjusted.

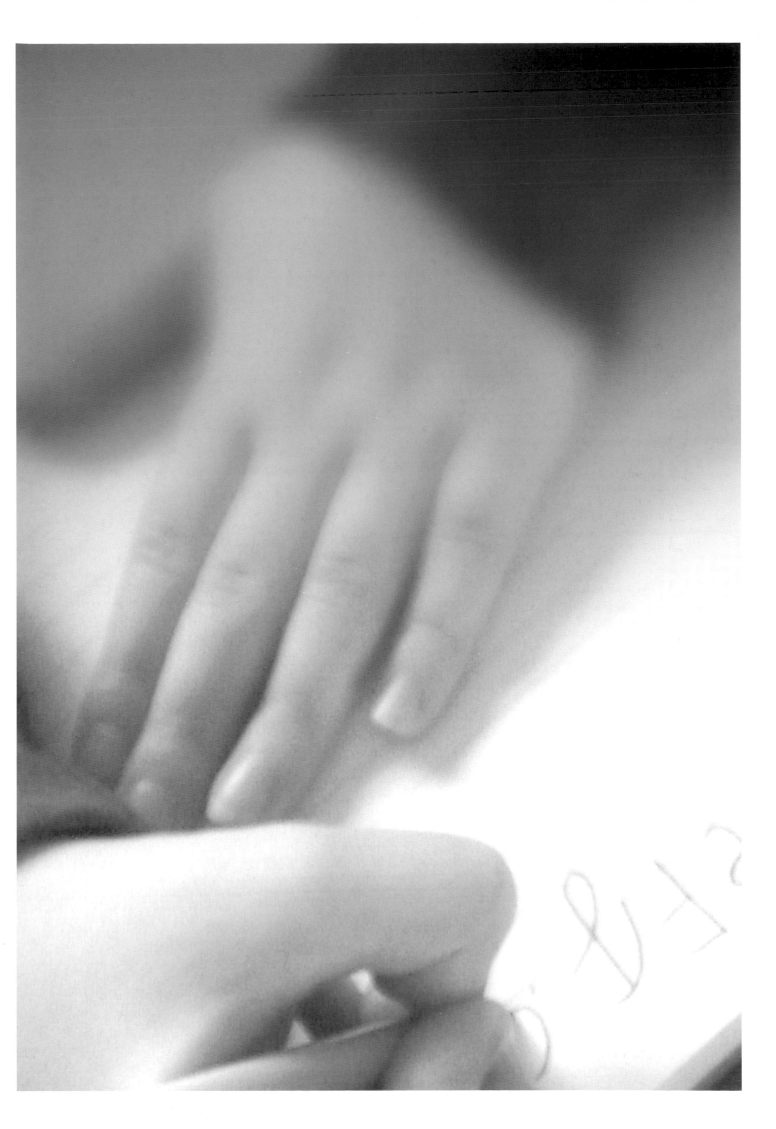

08 CHAPTER 1:
WHAT IS BIG WRITING?

 Chapter 1 reviews the key elements of raising standards in writing quickly and effectively through 'Big Writing', as described in the two previous publications.

Chapter 1 reviews the key elements of raising standards in writing quickly and effectively through 'Big Writing', as described in the two previous publications.

Big Writing is a totally new approach to the teaching of writing skills.

1.i   WHAT IS THE BIG WRITING PHILOSOPHY?
Instead of relying on analysis and knowledge of syntax to construct writing, 'Big Writing' is the development of the 'writing voice' through fast, fun, lively and predominantly oral activities.

MAKING PUPILS WHO DO NOT LIKE TO WRITE WRITE MORE WILL NOT MAKE THEM WRITE BETTER!

Pupils 'talk' the 'writing voice', both within a dedicated 'Big Writing' lesson and at as many other points during the week as time allows. The method is based on the premise that.

IF A CHILD CAN'T SAY IT, A CHILD CAN'T WRITE IT!

However, the 'writing voice' is not the same as the 'talking voice'. For example, it would be considered pompous to open a sentence with a participle in speech (an '...ing word' in 'Big Writing'), but it would 'score goals' if used in writing. Therefore the children enjoy making up sentences opening with '...ing words' orally and are told that if they do this when they do write, they will score goals.

BOYS LOVE TO TALK!

And....

WHAT'S GOOD FOR THE BOYS IS GOOD FOR THE GIRLS!
(See Chapter 7: 'The Difference Between Boys and Girls').

Children score 'training goals' for appropriate responses in the oral session.

If allowed, chocolate 'footballs' are a very good short-term incentive and make the lesson fun. They also play a significant part in re-motivating disaffected boys.

The writer is conscious of, and subscribes to, the healthy schools philosophy, however the use of chocolate or other treats is only ever recommended as a short term motivator, and the footballs may be 'forgotten' after a period of about eight weeks. If a school still feels, however, that it cannot subscribe to the use of sweets, grapes may be used.

When pupils go up a sub-level in writing, they have moved up the 'league table'. Many talented teachers actually make a league table, as illustrated in 'Quick Impact Strategies for Raising Standards in Writing'. Please note that the methods recommended for making the League Table do not allow identification of the level a child is at, and enable children of all abilities to be in any given column as it records movement between levels, not levels themselves.

MANY PUPILS, PARTICULARLY BOYS, ARE DISAFFECTED FROM WRITING
(see Chapter 7, 'The Difference between Boys and Girls').

The environmental changes, the pupil resources and the use of 'goals' are crucial aspects of the strategy, designed to give pupils the message that this approach is new and different, and may be regarded as a new beginning. (See Chapter 1.iii 'Environmental Changes for Big Writing'.)

1.ii   WHAT IS BIG WRITING – THE METHOD?
Big Writing takes one a half hours a week, plus 'stocking fillers' (see 1.xi 'What Are Stocking Fillers?')

The time budget comes from the one hour that would traditionally have been literacy (or its equivalent) that day, plus half an hour that would have been devoted to extended writing at some point in the week.

The one and a half hours should be split exactly in half by morning playtime/break, creating two forty-five minute sessions.

 NB This will only be one hour divided into two thirty minute sessions in Year 1.

The first forty-five minute session is thirty-five minutes of fast, fun, lively oracy- based activities. There is then ten minutes for the pupils to 'consolidate their ideas' (finalise plans). The focus and text type will have been introduced the day before (see Chapter 1.viii, 'Planning for Big Writing') and as pupils enter the classroom at the beginning of 'Big Writing' they will have selected the planning format they wish to use from the five or more options ready at the side of the room.

In Big Writing the objective of the ten minutes planning time is not the production of an impressive plan, but rather to refocus the pupil's thoughts on the stimulus and text type for writing.

'Strategies for Immediate Impact on Writing Standards' includes exemplification of six different ways to plan.

These are:

Cartoon strips
Open, body and ending scaffold
Thought clouds
Lists – key characters, key settings, key events, key words to use
Mind maps
Thinking* (PTO)

(See also Appendix 4 'The 'Write on Track' Intervention')

📌 ***NB** If the pupil is clearly not ready to write when the second session begins, 'thinking' is probably not an appropriate method for her/him.

A range of planning methods should be taught explicitly within Key Stage 1 and children should always be given a choice of how to plan each week. Many children do not like planning. Giving a choice encourages engagement.

The second forty-five minutes is writing.

The following table summarises the key aspects of 'Big Writing'. All are explained in detail within this and other chapters.

🕐 TIME	➕ FOCUS
✏️ **Session 1** 'Big Writing' lesson	35 minutes of fast, fun, lively oracy based activities to develop the writing voice. 10 minutes to refocus and consolidate planning
✏️ **Session 2** 'Big Writing' lesson	45 minutes writing. Text type changes every week, (see 1.vii 'Changing the Text Type'). 10 minute time prompts built in as brain breaks and to support pupils in ensuring that VCOP is in use, (see Chapter 1.x 'What is the Role of the Teacher in Big Writing?')
✏️ **Stocking Fillers**	Frequent short sessions on VCOP throughout the week. 5 minutes for VCOP oral activities 10 to 15 minutes for up-levelling, 'stealing', 'Spot the Difference' or other games and activities, (see the Appendices to this publication plus 'Strategies for Immediate Impact on Writing Standards' 2003).
✏️ **10 minutes** 'Basic Skills' per day	Each day a lively, fun focus on one of five Basic Skills, (see Chapter 8, 'The Importance of Basic Skills'.)

1.iii ENVIRONMENTAL CHANGES FOR BIG WRITING

When the children re-enter the room after playtime/break, there should be three environmental changes:

- The lighting should have been dimmed. This is usually achieved by turning off one bank of lights or by closing the curtains or blinds. There is considerable evidence in research that pupils do not like the lighting as bright as many teachers have it and, furthermore, that the strip lighting found in many classrooms can be disruptive to behaviour and concentration for some pupils.

- A large aroma candle should be lit at the front. Whenever we have candles or a fire burning at home, we pause from time to time to gaze at the flame and reflect. If children take a 'brain break' while writing, they gaze at the candle flame, reflect and return to their work.

- Mozart should be playing on a stereo. This should be so soft that it cannot be heard unless the classroom is silent. There is considerable evidence in research that Mozart's music is synchronic with the creative process of writing.

These three environmental changes induce an almost 'electric' silence that the children love. This is being increasingly recognised by OFSTED and we have received copies of reports where inspectors describe the atmosphere of Big Writing as 'spiritual' (see Case Studies 3,9 and 10, Heaton Primary School, New Hall Junior, Infant and Nursery Community School and Wilsden Primary School).

Expect silence for writing and you will achieve it!

Tell pupils, the first week, that when they come back in after break it is 'Big Writing' time. They should move to their places in silence, be seated and let their writing 'pour out' onto their paper. Their materials for writing should be ready on their tables. Meet pupils at the door as they come in, and avoid speaking. Use a finger to the lips and a soft 'Shhh' if necessary to calm them as they enter. The changed atmosphere should do the rest. If a pupil still needs a quiet word this should be whispered and if necessary calmly suggest a change in the pupil's seating to encourage concentration. Young children or pupils with concentration difficulties may have independent 'quiet' activities on their table top in case they finish early. These might include an interesting and appropriate level book, a word search or other puzzle, or unfinished work from an earlier lesson.

Pupils still at the very early stages of writing (WL1, L1 and some at 2C) may wish to work in a separate area with an adult with whom they can discuss their work. However this should be regarded as an option and not an enforced withdrawal.

NB For Health and Safety:

The candle should be secured in a tin 'bucket' or planter, with rocks round it to ensure stability. It usually stands prominently on top of something very stable (sometimes the overhead projector), on a desk or stand at the front of the classroom. A table can be placed across the access route either side of the table (T format) to ensure pupils do not knock it as they move to their places.

PLEASE DO NOT UNDERESTIMATE THE IMPACT OF THESE ENVIRONMENTAL CHANGES (THE DIMMED LIGHTING, THE CANDLE, THE SOFT PLAYING OF MOZART AND THE PUPILS' SILENCE), WHICH SHOULD BE RESERVED FOR BIG WRITING ONLY.

Music may be used in other lessons but should not be the same music as used in Big Writing.

1.iv RESOURCES FOR BIG WRITING

During the break a teaching assistant and/or pupil helpers should support the teacher in preparing for the writing session. The only preparation the teacher MUST retain responsibility for is the security and lighting of the candle.

Four types of resources should be placed on each pupil's desk during the break:

• **The child's writing portfolio.** This should be a very special resource unlike ones previously used in lessons. The writer invests in 10 pocket display albums. These hold twenty pieces of writing back to back, more than the number of weeks in even the longest term. This ensures room for highlighted text at the back, from which the child can 'steal' language. The child's personal targets can be slipped in front of the front piece of writing. At the end of the term the writing can be removed. Each child can make an attractive cover in art, design and technology or ICT, and assemble the term's writing as a book of evidence, enabling the portfolio to be recycled.

• **A special pen.** The writer invests in roller balls, with a velvet textured body, to make the sensation of writing as pleasurable as possible. A named pupil is responsible for counting pens out and in, and ensuring all are properly 'closed' before being put away until the next week.

• **A piece of A4 lined paper with a pre-drawn margin (A5 for Year 1 only).** Please note, teachers should never edit on top of a child's writing, it is an intrusion and many pupils find it offensive. Put a small line under an aspect you wish to draw attention to and write in the margin. Do not focus on more than three items for improvement. Give written feedback on the writing below. Always focus on positives first, then always leave a 'next step' for continued improvement.

Pupils should be seated with a talk partner, and they should read the feedback on each other's writing together, and discuss it. *

• **Three 'goals'.** These should be fruit in the writing session (chocolate footballs are a popular incentive in the oral session, however the atmosphere for writing must be calm and peaceful, and further chocolate would be counter productive). Three grapes are ideal for most pupils. For the few who do not like grapes, provide slices of apple or segments of tangerine. These goals are for structure, ie length, detail and description (LDD). See Chapter 5.iv, 'Length, Detail and Description'.

 *NB The writer usually returns the marked or assessed work at a different time to Big Writing, usually the day before. Time for discussion with their Talk Partner is then built in at this time.

1. v TEXT TYPES

The text type should change each week in Big Writing.

This helps to embed the skills of using VCOP (see Chapter 1.ix, 'What is VCOP?'), in every piece of writing, regardless of text type. One of the disadvantages of the literacy strategy as most teachers teach it, is that it gives children the impression that specific skills are tied to particular text types. They do not believe they can use certain phrases or structures unless they are writing within that one text type.

Children should be taught VCOP as the Four Generic Targets, as outlined in the two previous books. A synopsis is provided in Chapter 1.ix. They should then be taught that generic skills MUST be used whenever they write.

The focus for Big Writing may be from another subject, and thus the forty-five minutes spent on writing can be counted from that time budget. For example:

• a newspaper report about a religious, historical or geographical event

• an explanation text for science, design and technology, PE or ICT

• a balanced argument for citizenship, PSHE, environmental geography or RE

This gives greater purpose to the writing, establishes strong cross-curricular links and frees up forty-five minutes of timetable time elsewhere for additional creativity.

1.vi   THE CHANT AS A 'HOOK'

Pupils should write less often, probably only once or at most twice a week, but ALWAYS at their 'best' level!

Many teachers have historically accepted low level writing in other subjects, especially in the foundation subjects. This gives pupils the hidden message that it is alright to write at low levels at certain times, we do not always have to show our 'best' skills. As a result, when under pressure in a testing situation, a child can slip into their lower level writing style because they are focusing so closely on the previously unseen stimulus.

We recommend that pupils are always required to write at their 'best' level. Before they write for any purpose they should chant the following;

"What have we got to remember? The VCOP!"

This chant is done as a VAK activity (visual, auditory and kinaesthetic) to reflect the three dominant learning styles. Pupils use both hands to make a 'V' shape as they say the 'V', the left hand to make a 'C' shape as they say 'C', both hands to make the 'O' shape as they say 'O' and both hands to make the 'P' shape as they say 'P'. Adults modelling should remember to reverse the 'P' and 'C' shapes so that they are visually correct for the children.

Dedicate the writing part of Big Writing to a different curricular subject and literacy text type each week, always expecting pupils to write to 'Big Writing' standards and in the appropriate atmosphere (see Chapter 1.iii, 'Environmental Changes for Big Writing'). If required a 'short piece' could be produced in another lesson for purpose, but again to Big Writing standards in the spirit of the Key Stage 2 shorter writing test and using the Big Writing chant as a hook to indicate expectation of high standards and evidence of VCOP.

'Hooks' are usually strategies for enabling pupils to quickly re-access earlier learning. They may be slogans, pneumonics, acronyms, catch phrases, chants or other, similar devices. Clearly the 'hook' must not be more complex or difficult to remember than the original learning we wish pupils to 'hook back into'. (See Chapter 7.i ' Making Connections').

Consistent use of the chant has proved a highly effective hook for achieving consistency of standards in different text types and in different writing opportunities. It also plays a significant role in addressing 'summer dip' (see 'Raising Standards in Writing', 'Strategies for Immediate Impact on Writing Standards' and Chapter 2.vi, 'What Are the Timing and Purposes of Targeted Assessment Tasks?')

In September 2004 the writer received a telephone call from the Head of English in The Grange School, Bradford. She asked for a quick summary of what VCOP meant and explained that many pupils who had just entered Year 7 were reminding each other to use VCOP. She had observed that the standard of writing on entry was better than in previous years.

1.vii   CHANGING THE TEXT TYPES

The following table gives an illustration for how the changing of the text type on a weekly basis can be worked alongside the National Literacy Strategy Units of Work if they are in use. Teachers are reminded that the text type under study within the NLS Unit should not be the focus of whole-text writing until the completion of the period of research and analysis required within the unit. Thus, during the interim weeks previously studied text types can be recycled as the focus for 'Big Writing.

Linking the NLS Unit plans with Big Writing
Based on the Year 2 Term 1 NLS Units

⏱ WEEK	📋 NLS Unit Plan	➕ Possible 'Big Writing' text type
1	Narrative 1	Revisit text type – Recount (Y1 T3)
2	Narrative 1	NLS Unit plan outcome – oral & written retell
3	Non-fiction 1: Instructions	Revisit text type – Recount (Y1 T3)
4	Non-fiction 1: Instructions	NLS Unit plan outcome- simple instructions
5	Poetry	Revisit text type – Narrative: Story with simple setting (Y1 T3)
6	Poetry	NLS Unit plan outcome – class anthology, poems
7	Narrative 2	Revisit text type – Informal letter to a character or cross–curricular writing
8	Narrative 2	NLS Unit plan outcome – story
9	Non-fiction 2: Instructions	Revisit text type – Informal letter to a friend or cross-curricular writing, (could be narrative, instructions, recount or poem)
10	Non-fiction 2: Instructions	NLS Unit plan outcome – instructions containing diagrams

Based on an actual NLS Year 2 Unit Plan, Michelle Wraith (Literacy and Big Writing Consultant), September 2004

By Year 6 the full text range should have been taught and now it is possible for all text types to be 'recycled' through Big Writing approximately once a half term. This is a powerful model that keeps all text types 'on the front burner' instead of forgotten in a previous term or year.

1.viii   PLANNING FOR BIG WRITING

The text type and context/stimulus should be introduced the afternoon before Big Writing, in fifteen minutes as close as possible to the end of the day (preferably before or after 'story'). Divide the fifteen minutes roughly in half:

1. Discuss the stimulus e.g. a letter home from one of the crew on the Santa Maria sailing across the Atlantic Ocean in 1492, reliving the event.

2. Discuss the text type. Show a visual prompt of the characteristics, preferably the same visual as used when the text type was taught originally. Many schools have laminated cards, posters or Big Books of text types. Showing the visual enables pupils to 'hook in' or make the links easily. (See Chapter 7.i 'Making Connections'). Briefly review the characteristics. Display the visual at the front of the classroom for the next day. Ideally all classes should use the same resources in order to provide the most effective hooks.

Give the stimulus / context as homework. This should ALWAYS be predominantly through talk. Ask the children to talk to as many people as they can about what it might be like to be the person who is the subject of the writing, or how people might feel about the event etcetera. Ask them to consider as many viewpoints as possible and to start collecting ideas and potential words and phrases in their heads. A short note might be sent home to explain the focus of the 'talk' homework.

If a child has no-one to talk to, ask them to sit and think for five minutes, and to draw a stick-man picture of an aspect of the event, or of the person who is the subject. Tell them this will embed the subject in their memory and their sub-conscious will work on it during the night.

TELL CHILDREN ABOUT THE POWER OF THE SUB-CONSCIOUS!

Illustrate the power of the sub-conscious by asking pupils if they have ever seen their mother or another adult trying to remember a person's or place name. The adult may say it will 'come to them later'. Then, very often several hours later, when they have forgotten that they were trying to remember it, they suddenly say, 'Oh! I have just remembered.....' Tell the children this is because the sub-conscious continues to search on through the myriad of bits of information in the memory, and when it at last finds the answer it pops it into the conscious and the person remembers.

Explain to children that our sub-conscious is a powerful tool that can work for us and help us in our planning. It will work on for us when our conscious mind has moved on to other things.

1.ix   WHAT IS VCOP?

VCOP are the four generic targets identified in the process of assessing large volumes of writing at one time in 'the school in the desert' where many ideas were consolidated and developed (see 'Raising Standards in Writing' 2002).

The writer identified these four aspects of writing as the ones that consistently impacted on voice and style and continued to develop as pupils moved through the levels and sub-levels up to Level 5, and in some cases beyond, through increased repertoire and the degree of the factor of ambition. Other aspects of writing develop for a period and then become 'maintenance only' when they reach an optimum level, for example, handwriting and phonics.

The following table summarises VCOP (see also 'Raising Standards in Writing' 2002 and 'Strategies for Immediate Impact on Writing Standards' 2003).

✚ VCOP	💬 SUMMARY
VOCABULARY	The range of ambitious vocabulary a pupil knows; 'WOW' words.
CONNECTIVES	The range of ways pupils have for joining ideas, phrases and sentences
OPENERS	The strategies pupils have for opening sentences, and especially the 3 key openers: connectives, 'ly' words and 'ing' words.
PUNCTUATION	The range of punctuation a pupil can use and the accuracy with which they use it.

1.x WHAT IS THE ROLE OF THE TEACHER DURING BIG WRITING?

During the second session, when pupils are actually writing, the teacher sits quietly, maintaining but not disturbing the deep concentration that will have been achieved. However, s/he does have an important role to play through the giving of 'time prompts'. These have two functions:

1. To provide ten minute 'brain breaks', reflecting what we know about children's capacity to concentrate (see Chapter 6.iii 'The Impact of What We Know About Concentration Spans').

2. To prompt pupils to build in VCOP.

A clock should be visible to all pupils, preferably above the teaching board. Ideally it should either be colour coded into ten minute blocks, or have markers at the ten minute blocks, commencing at the time the writing session would normally start. Thus if pupils come in from break at 11.15 am, the markings would start at 11.20, and occur again at 11.30, 11.40, 11.50 and 12.00 noon.

The time prompts are given as follows:

11.30 "You have had ten minutes. Count how many sorts of punctuation you have used." (NB Pupils must be taught to count 'sorts of' and not 'pieces of'.)

11.40 "You have had twenty minutes. How many ambitious words/wow words have you used?"

11.50 "You have had thirty minutes. Look at your openers. Have you opened with connectives? Have you opened with 'ly' words? Have you opened with 'ing' words?"

12.00 "You have five minutes left."
In the early weeks, the time prompts may be extended by reminding pupils that they should try to use at least three of a particular aspect, or asking for examples of what children have used, to reinforce the message for less able pupils.

By April of each year the teacher can reduce the level of support by saying;

11.30 "You have had ten minutes. What would I be asking you now? Well done – how many sorts of punctuation have you used?"

11.40 "You have had twenty minutes. What would I be asking you now? Well done – how many wow words have you used?"

11.50 "You have had thirty minutes. What would I be asking you now? Well done – look at your openers. Have you used....?"

12.00 "You have five minutes left."

By April of Year 6 pupils should be using the clock independently to manage time. In the test only a half time prompt can normally be given. Pupils should know that by the half way prompt they should have done the first two and will have one more to do. (See Case Study 11; 'The British School, Tokyo')

1.xi WHAT ARE STOCKING FILLERS?

All the oral activities of the first session are potential stocking fillers (see Appendix 2).

Teachers should take advantage of the fact that many lessons could usefully end five or more minutes before they actually do. Frequently in the afternoons, particularly in foundation subjects such as geography, history and Religious Education, many pupils spend too long on activities. We must remember that most children have a great capacity for making an activity last as long as the time provided, when they could actually have finished it long before.

Every day teachers should aim to finish at least one lesson five minutes before the end of the session and do some of the oral VCOP activities. Additional quick activities can be done while getting changed or waiting for the hall for P.E. or while lining up for assembly. At least twice a week ten minute or more slots should be created for 'up-levelling' simple sentences or one of Marmaduke's paragraphs (see Chapter 8.viii 'What is the Imaginary Friend?')

Furthermore, whenever text is read with or to pupils, adults should always look for opportunities to 'steal' new examples of VCOP. Having pre-scanned the text, the adult might say, 'Just before we read this there is a fantastic new 'wow' word here,' or 'As I read this to you see if you can spot a great new opening here.' The use of the word 'steal' is a conscious choice and should be explained to children as they mature. It is a crucial element of giving pupils ownership so that they will retain and use the word freely in a range of contexts. (See also Chapter 4.iv, 'Why Are We Stealing?')

These quick but frequent embedding activities are called 'stocking fillers'.

**"Music turned down low,
Candles really glow.
Our Big Writing Day each week –
To eat five goals we seek.
We're raring to go!!!!"**

Jenna and Jahsiah
Year 6, Crossley Hall Primary School, Bradford.

16 CHAPTER 2:
THE LONG TERM STRATEGY

 Chapter 2 reviews the implementation of the Long Term Strategy.

2.i   WHAT IS THE LONG TERM STRATEGY?

The elements of the Long Term Strategy are:

- the compilation of an evidence base showing all pupils in the school making progress

- tracking of pupils' progress and development of writing

- evidence of pupils' movement through sub-levels and levels in writing

- monitoring of teachers' use of agreed strategies for raising standards in writing

- monitoring of progress towards cohort and whole school targets for writing

- involving pupils in their own learning and the assessment process (assessment for learning)

The long term strategy is based on administration of four formal assessments each academic year, (Targeted Assessment Tasks, generally abbreviated to 'TATs'). Pupils from Year 1 to Year 6 should be required to produce a piece of unsupported writing within a timed period. During the first year of TATs it is recommended that the writing should be within the context of a letter. (See below 'Why Use A Letter For Formal TAT Assessments?')

Each TAT should be formally assessed using the Criterion Scale for assessment, and should be awarded a sub-level of achievement, a long term numerical target for achievement by the end of a set period, (usually a term or a year) and three small-step targets that will result in the pupil moving forward immediately towards their numerical target.

Please note that for schools in 'category', (Special Measures / Serious Weaknesses) evidence of half termly assessment and tracking may be required. This system equally meets these needs.

2.ii   WHY USE A LETTER FOR FORMAL TAT ASSESSMENTS?

Unless we compare like with like, fluctuations in achievement will be found in the first year until the four generic skills are embedded. Currently, when children change text types their sub-level of achievement often fluctuates. This is because they have varying understanding of, and response to, different text types. This might be due to their variable attitude to learning at the time of teaching, the teacher's variable enthusiasm towards different text types, clarity of teaching for different text types, or grasp of the characteristics of different text types. It could also be due to variable response of either adults in delivering or in pupils reacting to the stimulus for writing.

It is recommended that a letter be used as the context for TATs, at least for the first year. The following are the reasons for this:

1. Until Big Writing is embedded, it is most useful to compare 'like with like'. As previously stated, pupils' achievement is currently different when they are writing in different text types. If the text type is changed for each assessment scores will fluctuate and tracking will be insecure. After a year of Big Writing, VCOP is embedded in all text types. This is further enhanced by the weekly change of text type in the lessons (see Chapter 1.vii 'Changing the Text Types').

2. Letters are currently one of the text types that pupils tend to find less stimulating, and they often produce lower level writing in response. If a child can perform well in a letter they can perform well in most other text types.

3. Letters lend themselves to embracing the characteristics of a second text type, thus enabling a doubly secure assessment of certain criteria. Examples of this are provided in the Appendix of 'Strategies for Immediate Impact on Writing Standards' 2003, where there is a pure narrative letter, an explanation text within a letter, a report within a letter and a persuasive letter.

4. Letters enable secure judgements on several criteria that some other text types may not. For example, those relating to structure and organisation, awareness of audience and adaptation.

Ensure the purpose for the letter is interesting and stimulating. The following exemplify some of the types of ideas for letter writing that pupils have enjoyed in the past:

- narrative writing in the role of an exciting character from a popular story or film, e.g. Harry Potter or Spiderman

- a letter of complaint to the local council with regard to a proposal to build a chicken or pig farm on the school's playing field. This could include argument or balanced argument

- a persuasive letter from a famous football club manager, attempting to lure a named famous player to his team

- an explanation letter to a member of staff with a sense of humour (preferably yourself!) saying why he or she is about to be fired

2.iii WHAT IS THE PROCESS FOR MANAGEMENT AND TRACKING THROUGH THE LONG TERM STRATEGY?

The strategy should be managed by one 'driver' supported by at least one Senior Manager, or a second member of SMT if the 'driver' is also a Senior Manager. If writing is an urgent priority of the school the whole SMT will wish to be involved in the process through regular information sessions and scrutiny of the trackers.

The 'driver' is supported by at least one other adult who is not normally a member of the teaching force, (workforce remodelling). This person may be a Teaching Assistant, a governor, a volunteer parent or grandparent, a retired member of the profession or an alternative respected member of the community. The person should be able to respect confidentiality and work systematically.

Data presentation may be managed by this support adult OR another support adult e.g. a member of the ICT support team, or a member of the office staff.

The elements of the process:

1. The 'driver' receives photocopies of assessed writing TATs and updated trackers from each class teacher, and supervises the process of compilation of the school's evidence base.

2. TATs are organised into uni-lever ring binders by class, with dividers between each class. There is then a plastic pocket for each pupil, labelled clearly with his/her name and date of birth. Further information may include first language and entry to this school.

3. The updated tracker is inserted after the divider, (See Case Study 6 for model tracker, 'All Saints Primary School, Isle of Wight').

4. The baseline is inserted in the pupil's pocket, facing backwards. It is never removed.

5. Each following TAT is inserted on top of the previous one facing forwards. In order to avoid plastic pockets becoming over full and splitting the following process should be applied. As the December TAT of the current year is inserted, the previous December one should be removed. As the March TAT is inserted, the previous March one should be removed. The baseline and May TATs for all years are never removed, thus providing an excellent record of a pupil's progress in writing. By Year 6 a pupil who has been doing Big Writing since Reception will have his baseline (facing backwards), then his Year 1 May TAT, his Year 2 May TAT, his Year 3 May TAT, his Year 4 May TAT, his Year 5 May TAT and his Year 6 December and March TATs. The final insertion will be a copy of his SAT longer writing task.

6. The driver and SMT track progress in Value Added (VA) terms, measured in sub-levels. e.g. +2 = 2 sub-levels moved; +4 = 4 sub-levels moved since the last point of assessment.

7. Monitoring through trackers enables identification of pupils making excellent progress and pupils making little or no apparent progress, plus classes where the strategy is seemingly having excellent impact. Might this be a potential 'lead teacher'/peer coach for other colleagues?

8. Where there appears to be excellent progress, the driver and colleagues examine the evidence in the pupil's pocket. Is this an opportunity to celebrate with staff?

9. Where there appears to be little or no progress, the driver and colleagues examine the evidence in the pupil's pocket. Should the teacher be offered support? Is the child actually moving, but at a slower pace because of significant special need?

10. Where a whole class does not appear to be making similar patterns of progress to other classes, should the teacher be offered support?

11. Where children are recognised to be consistently on a significantly slower journey than peers, should the evidence be brought to a whole staff meeting to enable a pooling of all ideas, and to develop a shared understanding of the issues so that the maximum potential progress over time can be guaranteed.

12. The entire process should be managed transparently and with constant, clear feedback to all.

13. The driver and SMT should plan the TATs, identifying the text type and stimulus **ENSURING THAT IT WILL BE APPROPRIATE, LIVELY AND INTERESTING TO MOTIVATE PUPILS**, and communicate the time frame within which it should be completed.

14. SMT should plan and facilitate a moderation session in order for staff to standardise their judgements and moderate pre-selected pieces that have caused difficulties for individual teachers and/or year teams because they are on a threshold. (See 2.v 'How Do We Manage Standardisation of Judgements?')

15. SMT should ensure that Big Writing is appropriately timetabled and implemented every week.

2.iv WHAT IS THE PROCESS FOR MANAGING THE LONG TERM STRATEGY IN THE CLASSROOM?

The following is the recommended process for management of the Long Term Strategy:

1. The teacher ensures that she/he is fully informed on the school's expectation for text type, stimulus and time scale for each TAT, and endeavours to meet these requirements.

2. The teacher enables pupils to achieve their best through organising the classroom and resources in the way most conducive for pupils to achieve their maximum potential, and manages the assessment in a positive and calm atmosphere, free from stress.

3. The teacher* assesses each piece of writing against the Criterion Scale, recording her/his assessment in terms of ticks (definite evidence), dots (inconclusive but may be) and crosses (no evidence at all), down the left hand margin of the paper. (NB TATs should be completed on uniform sheets of lined paper with a pre-drawn margin – A5 for Year 1 and A4 for Years 2 to 6.)

4. The teacher participates in staff moderation sessions to ensure standardised judgements. (See Chapter 2.v, 'How Do We Manage Standardisation of Judgements?')

5. The teacher updates the appropriate column on the tracker, calculating and recording the VA in the appropriate column, or supervises successful completion of this process by a trusted adult.

6. The teacher manages the process of photocopying all TATs and the tracker, and ensures a copy of all scripts and the tracker are sent to the driver.

7. The teacher supervises the organisation of the class portfolio, (usually a ring binder) with assessed work inserted into a named pocket that exactly duplicates that in the school evidence base.

NB THE NUMERICAL JUDGEMENT SHOULD BE RUBBED OFF THE COPY IN THE CLASS PORTFOLIO.
(See Chapter 4.v 'What Does Each Level Look Like?').

8. The class portfolio should be sent to the next teacher when the class moves at the end of an academic year.

9. When the December and March scripts are inserted in the portfolio, the December and March scripts from the previous year should be removed to ensure pockets do not become over full. The original baseline and the final assessment of the year (May) are never removed from the portfolio, so that a permanent evidence base of the pupil's annual progress is retained. (See Chapter 2.iii 'What is the Process for Management and Tracking through the Long Term Strategy?').

*In some schools a Teaching Assistant has proved to be an excellent assessor with training, and has taken on that role for the whole school, with appropriate release time to do so. The class teacher should second-assess each script and the Literacy Co-ordinator and driver/s should randomly 'second assess' to ensure validity.

2.v HOW DO WE MANAGE STANDARDISATION OF JUDGEMENTS?

The following is a simple but effective process for management of standardisation:

• Once a half term (or a month if a high priority) colleagues are asked to bring their Criterion Scale and a pencil to the staff meeting.

• A pre-selected piece of writing is on each chair in the staff room. In the early days it is most useful to regularly target Level 2 as this is the crucial level where pupils labelled as having special needs are 'trapped' (see 7.v 'The Joshua Case Study Revisited'). In addition, many teachers over assess, awarding a Level 3 or even 4 to a piece that has not yet met the requirements of Level 2B or 2A, because they are not aware of the complexity of development at this stage.

• As staff settle, they spend up to five minutes (maximum) assessing the piece. Colleagues should be encouraged to read carefully, but then work quickly through the criteria for the target level, assessing down the margin of the piece through the use of ticks (definitely can), dots (a small amount of evidence but not secure), or crosses (no evidence shown here). (See 'Raising Standards in Writing' 2002 and 'Strategies for Immediate Impact on Writing Standards' 2003).

• A further five minutes is spent in discussion to agree a whole staff judgement. The piece must have been pre-assessed by at least two managers who are confident and accurate assessors in order to ensure authoritative justification and exemplification in the case of ongoing differing opinions.

• The staff meeting now proceeds as usual.

• Once a term or twice yearly a longer session involving several pieces at different levels should be organised. This might be forty-five minutes of a staff meeting or one session on an in-service training day.

2.vi WHAT ARE THE TIMING AND PURPOSES OF TARGETED ASSESSMENT TASKS (TATs)?

TATs are normally conducted at the following points of the academic year in all classes from Year 1 to Year 6:

1. A baseline piece executed at the point at which the school adopts the strategy. This is used to identify the initial long term target for each pupil, to examine the implications for existing whole-school and cohort targets and also to identify the first precise short term targets for communication to, and discussion with, students. The original baseline remains in the child's plastic pocket until the child leaves the school. It should be at the back of the pocket and turned backwards, so that a quick comparison can be made between the child's writing at the commencement of tracking, and their latest piece.

2. Termly assessments in December, March and May. These assessment points may need adjustment in the first year of the strategy only, depending on the timing of the first baseline. e.g. if the baseline is conducted in November because awareness has just been raised, the assessments may be adjusted to January or mid-Spring Term, followed by one more in May.

3. A further assessment at the beginning of each academic year (September) to identify 'summer dip'. The first publication, 'Raising Standards in Writing' 2002 exemplifies and explains 'summer dip' in detail, but it is crucial to mention here that research shows that more than 50% of every class drop back during the summer holiday, and that it is not possible to predict who they will be.

2.vii WHAT CAN WE DO ABOUT SUMMER DIP?

The September assessment will identify all pupils who have 'dropped back' over the summer break. Indeed, the writer has a large body of evidence that the drop back begins immediately after the May tests are finished in many classrooms. This is because the skills are not embedded until most writers are working consistently at a high Level 4 or Level 5 or if a child is very young. If pupils do not use the skills regularly they can regress.

Some children who do not appear to have any home or environmental benefits to complement and sustain the process, may maintain or even improve standards during the holiday, while some who appear to have everything that is regarded as complementing the process (e.g. bedtime story, many opportunities to read, positive reading and writing role models and a home rich in extended language) can still drop back. This assessment should NOT be included in the main evidence base as it will distort the Value Added trail, but should be retained separately.

It is not unusual to find pupils who have not only 'dropped back' during the summer, but who are actually right back where they were the September before. (See 'Raising Standards in Writing' 2002).

A teacher needs to have a discreet discussion with every child who has been shown to have dropped back during the summer. The pupil should be shown the last piece of writing done for the previous teacher (usually in the May) which will be in the portfolio that has been sent up with the class. It should be compared with the piece written in September and the pupil should be asked to 'Spot the Difference' (one of the VCOP activities of 'Big Writing'). The pupil should be able to describe the difference, for example saying, "LDD and VCOP" when asked what they have 'forgotten' to use. (See Chapter 5.iv, 'Length, Detail and Description').

The teacher then acknowledges to the class that many have 'dropped back' during the long break, and says that this is alright, however, now everyone needs to get back to where they were by the end of last year. Pupils are given two choices. They may either have the first piece of writing back and 'up-level' it, or they may wait until the next time they write and 'up-level' then. Whichever the choice is, the teacher must ensure that all pupils are back to the level they were writing at the previous May, by the beginning of October so that they can move forward towards the targets that have been set for them.

**"Big Writing is close to our heart
So do come along and take part.
You'll reach higher levels
And enjoy super revels
By blowing yourself off the chart!**

Rachel and Alex
Year 5, Crossley Hall Primary School, Bradford.

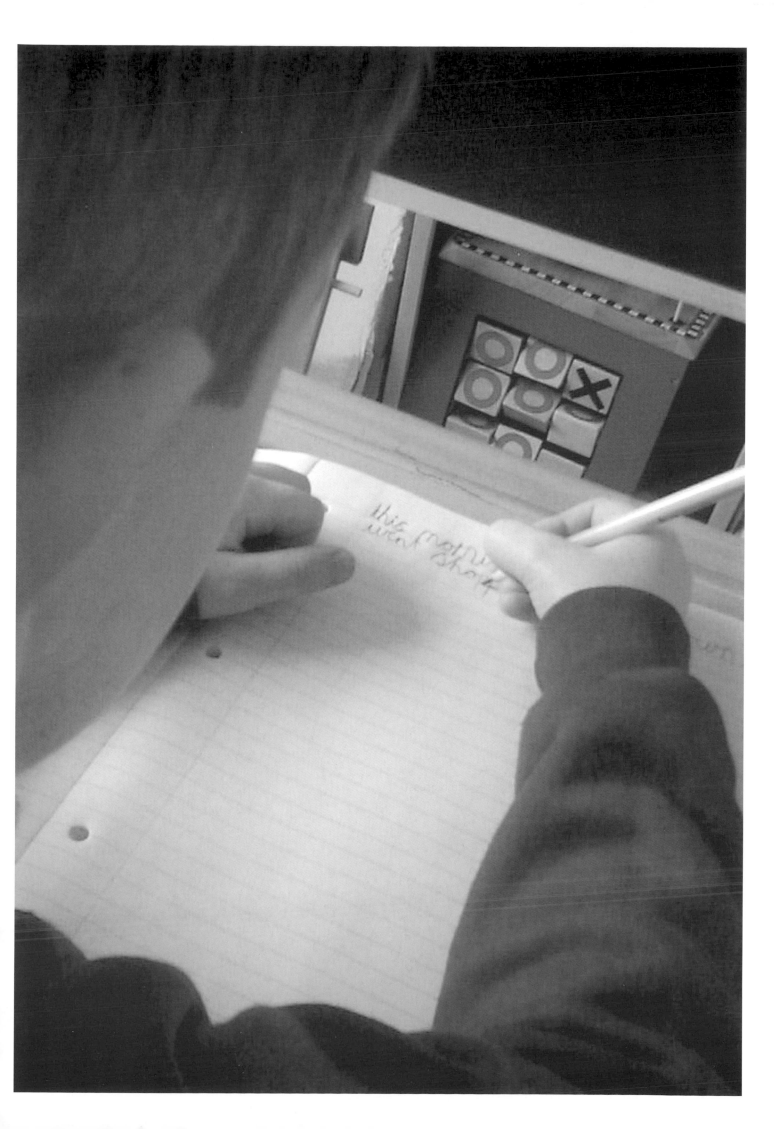

22 CHAPTER 3:
THE CONTRIBUTION OF THE FOUNDATION STAGE TO BIG WRITING

 Chapter 3 gives an overview of the role of the Foundation Stage in language development and its contribution to Big Writing, including the contribution of 'talking posh'. It also includes an interesting Case Study from Germany.

We do not advise formal writing lessons before children are six years old (see also Chapter 7.ii 'Starting Schooling'). We believe learning for pre-sixes should be about young children learning about life, the world around them and social skills through play. However, we recognise that there are pressures on adults working in the Foundation Stage to start the reading, writing and number journeys. This should be done through predominantly self-selected learning opportunities in a stimulating, warm and caring environment with constant praise.

Children who are reluctant to engage with these basic academic skills before the age of six should be offered a wide range of exciting opportunities and constant encouragement and support, but should not be placed under pressure. Creative adults provide writing opportunities that include a wide range of mark making materials, finger paint, working in damp sand, white wash brushes and water on walls outside, pastry and modelling materials, magnetic and other commercial alphabets and so on.

NB Some young children are ready to learn to write at four and five years old and these children should not be deprived of their entitlement. However, writing should always be an optional and pleasurable opportunity for them. (See 3.v 'How Did He Do That?')

The key roles of the Foundation Stage in writing are:

- The development of extended speech and encouragement of all children to be confident, articulate talkers. Young children who grow up in homes with restricted codes of speech should be constantly encouraged to talk. Asking them to use the 'because' word will give them quick success in providing extended answers (see below).

- Introduction of early oral VCOP activities, particularly focusing on 'wow' words, openers and connectives.

3.i ENCOURAGING EXTENDED SENTENCES
The most successful Early Years practitioners have a great talent for having seemingly unplanned and 'idle' conversations, engaging young children as they enjoy rich and stimulating learning opportunities. Some remarkable learning takes place through these conversations.

When a young child answers a question or offers a comment with one word or a short phrase, say to the child, "Can you say why? Can you use the 'because' word please?" Then say, "Can you put those two parts together please?" Always model for a child who is unsure.

 Examples may look like this:

Teacher; "What happened to the bed?"
Child; "Goldilocks broke it."
Teacher; "Can you say why? Can you use the 'because' word please?"
Child; "Because she was too heavy for it."
Teacher; "Can you put those two parts together please?"
Child; "Goldilocks broke it because she was too heavy for it."
Teacher; "Well done, that's a very good extended sentence."

In the beginning some children will naturally need help in putting the two parts together. If this is modelled through different children several times a day (at apparently random moments) most days of the week, children will soon grow confident in extending sentences.

Any time a young child voluntarily uses an extended sentence, he or she should be praised. If extended sentences are the 'norm', promote complex sentences through 'posh' talk. (See Chapter 8.vii, 'What Is 'Talking Posh'?').

3.ii 'WOW' WORDS
Fill young children's lives with rich vocabulary. We frequently have too low an expectation of the degree of 'ambitiousness' that a four year old can cope with.

Heaton Primary School (see Case Study 3) filled the lives of their children with rich vocabulary, to the extent that a four year old informed the Registered Inspector leading the school's OFSTED inspection that his briefcase was 'dilapidated'. Furthermore, when he asked what the word meant, the child was able to tell him.

Providing young children can pronounce the word, they can learn, own and use it with good teaching. The teacher must provide a range of appropriate models for the word (demonstrating in three or more different ways for most verbs and adverbs, and providing three or more actual artefacts or pictorial representations for most adjectives and nouns). It is essential that multiple models are provided, otherwise children are likely to associate the meaning with that example only.

When children can pronounce the word and say what it means they should 'play' with the word in the same way as older children will be doing. This is usually through oral application such as;

"Who can make me up a sentence with _____ in?"

Or "Which of our 'wow' words would be good in this sentence?"

Anytime a young child voluntarily uses a 'wow' word he or she should be praised.

3.iii   OPENERS AND CONNECTIVES

Preparation for becoming writers can be achieved through fun 'playing' with a range of openers and connectives within oral activities (see Appendix 2).

As young children grow in confidence at extending sentences, widen the range of connectives. In speech four year olds can comfortably operate connectives from both Levels 2 and 3, including and, but, so, or, then, if, when, because, before and after, and may continue to add connectives such as if only, as well as, also and plus.

Play 'games' such as;

"Which of these two connectives would fit best between these two sentences?"

"How is the meaning different when I use this connective or that connective?"

"Can you make up a sentence beginning with......?"

Focus on three sorts of openers in 'posh' talk which can be fun and often are done through role play. The three quick impact openers are:

• Opening with connectives

• Opening with 'ly' words

• Opening with 'ing' words

For very young children skillful practitioners often make these games appear like further 'idle' conversations that are going on while children are learning social skills and about the world through play. They can then be built on later, when involved in reading and shared writing activities.

Any time a young child voluntarily uses an interesting opener or connective, he or she should be praised.

3.iv   TALKING THE 'WRITING VOICE'

Even very young children within the Foundation Stage can enjoy 'talking the writing voice', and making up higher order sentences and phrases together can be small stocking fillers within the Reception classroom.

 For example:

Adult;   "Who can make me up a sentence beginning with 'When'?"

Child 1; "When I came to school I saw a squirrel."

Adult;   "Who can put me a WOW word into that sentence?"

Child 2; "When I STROLLED to school I saw a squirrel."

Adult;   "Who can put a second WOW word into our sentence?"

Child 3; "When I strolled to school I saw a golden squirrel."

An adult may scribe these sentences and display them as 'Our Big Writing' or 'Our WOW sentences'.

Drawing parents' attention to these activities, and explaining 'wow' words, openers and connectives to parents enables them to build onto this work as they walk to school, walk around the supermarket together or at meal times and bath times.

IT IS IMPORTANT THAT THESE ACTIVITIES ARE ONLY DONE FOR A FEW MINUTES AT A TIME AND REMAIN LIGHT HEARTED AND FUN FOR ALL CHILDREN!

YOUNG CHILDREN SHOULD BE ENCOURAGED TO TALK AS THEY LEARN!

3.v: HOW DID HE DO THAT?
CASE STUDY 1: BRITISH ARMY SCHOOL – BISHOPSPARK, GERMANY

Having clearly stated the writer's commitment to best practice in the Foundation Stage, she recently had the privilege of meeting an extremely talented teacher in Germany (British Army School – Bishopspark) who has achieved amazing results with his children of Reception age.

Steve Jessop attended the 'Raising Standards in Writing' conference in Celle, Germany, April 2005 arranged by Bill Aylett, head teacher of the Montgomery School. Steve had been teaching his class through Big Writing since purchasing the book, 'Strategies for Immediate Impact on Writing Standards' in 2004.

Having met the writer in Celle, he forwarded 16 samples of Reception pupils' writing and the following are edited excerpts from his accompanying letter:

✎ **Dear Ros,   24.04.05**
Thank you for a cracking conference in Celle last week. Talked to lots of people since and they were all very positive – just hope they get kinaesthetic and actually do it!

We've been implementing various aspects of your approach from Year 1 to Year 4 (first school) and are still developing it.

Ros, I hope you don't mind but I'd like to take issue on just one point – your suggestion that we hold back at Reception / Foundation Stage. I know where you are coming from but... my worry is that it feeds lower expectations of the 'they're only little' brigade sometimes found amongst Foundation Stage teachers and leaders.

Over here we have some fantastic advantages with virtually 100% two parent families, 100% employment, far less apathy, wonderful physical and human resources, one term intake and very favourable class sizes. However families are of very mixed backgrounds as one would expect in the army.
I have forwarded you examples of work done with my last Reception class which was pre the introduction of the NLS in the Foundation Stage. This was produced from a mixed catchment of lower and higher ranks with high mobility. The selections are all from children who were in the class long term. At that time we had nowhere near the resources and copying facilities we have now.

This standard of work stemmed from, most importantly of all, HIGH EXPECTATIONS brought about by several factors, not least a vested interest in my own children's development (or lack of it) and also the benefit of having started out as a Year 3 teacher in Sunny Scunny with appalling standards in all aspects of literacy, and gradually working my way 'down' to Reception over the next four to five years.

Obviously high expectations are just hot air unless we 'get kinaesthetic' – which manifests itself in the introduction and 'scientifically' developed delivery of the key word accessing skills you identify in the first section in your 'Progression in Teaching and Learning' page 9 in your 'purple' book. (I can't spell 'aubergine' – or can I?)

You can see why I like your stuff now. It confirms what I've always held dear myself. Are you sure you did not pinch it from me?

Also, and crucially, this structured approach was underpinned by a very activity / child-centred approach which capitalised upon children's immediate experiences, (school, family etcetera) and you will see aspects of this coming through in the children's writing. The context of the writing was a letter to their next teacher in Year 1. It was their first draft, having brain stormed words and utilised my patented 'sentence system' for preparation.

It's worth noting that the boys are as good as the girls and the quality was achieved two years in a row. The message here is not 'look how good these are' but please don't under estimate the 'ankle biters' and MORE IMPORTANTLY the positive effect they can have in raising the expectations of teachers in Year 1 and beyond.'

Sorry to go on a bit! The sad thing is I am as passionate about this as I was when I started and it was a real

inspiration to see you also doing it with such passion…. And you in your late forties!** It made me realise I'll probably never end up cynical or apathetic either – and we don't have to be 'posh 'uns' to boot to help the children 'get there'.

Cheers Ros,

Steve Jessop

PS Do have other hobbies – train spotting, twitching, collecting anoraks etcetera…

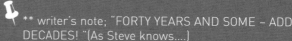 ** writer's note; "FORTY YEARS AND SOME – ADD DECADES! "(As Steve knows….)

The following are a summary of the main strategies Steve has developed, as gleaned from a brief exchange of e-mails:

- use of Big Writing Targets as individual targets
- activity based, fun ways of promoting VCOP
- a structured, balanced approach to developing all aspects of literacy
- lots of opportunities for real and play experiences
- motivational factors
- harnessing parental aspirations
- a 'scientific' approach to the basic aspects of reading ie using sight vocabulary as the main, initial springboard whilst simultaneously teaching phonic knowledge and skills for promoting the use of the initial letter sound and eventually blending and writing via segmentation
- a structured approach to phonics, sight vocabulary and handwriting firmly based in a VAK approach with the emphasis on ACTIVITY. Too many young children are at risk of developing piles in the literacy hour!
- high expectations and low tolerance of those with low ones
- no glass ceilings
- lots of fun!

Two samples of Steve's pupils' work follow.

The following are just two of the many equally impressive samples Steve sent in. The writer deliberately chose two boys' work.

Dear mrs Pursar
my name is Andrew
I like to lots
of writing.
my brother is back
nome with my
taddy and my
mummu.
I would like
to go backte Bruh
on a aeroplane
Love from
Andrew

Dear Mrs Purser

my name is Liam mc Caffi

my sister is grounded

Because she steals

biscuits. and she gives

me one. and then

she eats them all

I Like flying

and then I will

go home. I Like

playing in the play ground

Love LiAM

28 CHAPTER 4:
WHAT IS EFFECTIVE TARGET SETTING ?

 Chapter 4 explores issues around why it has historically often been difficult to identify small step targets for pupils in writing. It provides the Big Writing model for target setting.

4.i   WHAT'S THE PROBLEM?

Although the majority of primary teachers are now confident in setting medium and short term targets for a whole class, many teachers still struggle to identify effective small step target setting for individual pupils, to inform their personal progress and meet their personal needs within the day or week, particularly in the writing aspect of English.

The objectives in the National Curriculum, the National Strategies and the QCA Units of Study are often too broad to use as small step targets for children. They are usually goals to be achieved over a period of weeks or longer.

For effective pupil use, targets need to be achievable in the short term. Children need to know what to do tomorrow in order to make a difference and start moving towards their broader medium term objectives. Our schools' curricula rarely take objectives down to

small enough steps for teachers to use with children in this way.

Most young learners need sequential pathways of small steps that are achievable within the space of a lesson, a week or at most a fortnight.

Target setting is part of the assessment process. It is the most effective aspect of formative assessment, which is assessment that informs the next step for teaching. Most teachers use formative assessment well to plan the next lesson in order to meet the needs of the majority of the class. Target setting is the process of meeting the needs of each individual within the class. Assessment for Learning (A for L) is the process of involving the pupils in the assessment process and making them fully aware of what they need to do next in order to move forward, and what success looks like, so that each pupil has his or her own specific small–step targets that are understood and worked on.

4.ii   A Summary of the Three Forms of Assessment:

 Formative Assessment

Informs teaching:
Use of assessment in the short term, within a week usually, or even a lesson or piece of work, in order to plan the next step of teaching so that progression is ensured. It is informed by knowing how well pupils understood or could do the previous learning.

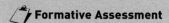 **Summative Assessment**

Makes a judgement on a pupil's attainment at a given point in time:
Use of assessment to make a specific judgment on the actual level of a pupil's performance, usually either by calculation based on accumulated short term assessments or through an assessment activity or test.

 Assessment for Learning

Involves pupils in their own learning and achievement:
Incorporates the principles of formative assessment, but explicitly involves the pupils in the process.

Pupils are enabled to know what success looks like, what skill levels are required and how to judge whether they have actually been successful. They are, therefore, able to form an opinion on the level of their own achievement, or that of another.

In addition, pupils have their own precise small-step targets matched to their individual needs that will ensure they are moving forward in a progressive way through the sub-levels of the National Curriculum, in order to move up the levels.

4.iii   WHY ARE SMALL STEPS OFTEN DIFFICULT TO IDENTIFY IN ENGLISH?

It is the adult's ability to identify and explain small enough steps for young learners to enable them to move forward confidently, that determines whether or not most pupils make best progress.

Big Writing is a method that incorporates the best practice in Assessment for Learning

Much has been written and said about use of Assessment for Learning to involve and empower children; however its impact on pupils' progress in writing within the subject of English is constrained by the difficulty of identifying logical steps that are small enough for children to be able to understand precisely what to do next and therefore to move forward confidently from step to step. Consequently, progress too often remains a 'hit and miss' affair in this aspect of English.

Small steps are often explicit in mathematics, particularly in number and measures. Most pupils are taught clearly in a sequential model for learning that enables steady forward progress towards expected levels of achievement. This model works particularly well for both boys and for bilingual learners operating in a foreign language. For both these groups, a coherent, logical and clear sequence is the preferred learning style.

Science works in a similar way with sequential content knowledge that can be taught formally, having value in its own right, or accessed and cognitively developed through an explicit process of investigative learning and research (behaving like a scientist, known as Attainment Target 1 in the original National Curriculum).

English is far more problematic.

There is a logical sequence within reading, handwriting, spelling – both sight words and phonics, analysis of grammar, and within the text types for writing, although not all schools and teachers use the most logical or sequential pathways to access young children to these skills. There has not been, however, a similar, explicit, structured pathway for developing the writing 'voice', (style and increasing sophistication) prior to the advent of Big Writing.

There is evidence that 'Big Writing' is, in fact, having an impact on the other aspects of English, and may actually support improvement in the problem solving aspects of mathematics and science. This is because children's understanding of the more subtle aspects of language improves through the 'games' using VCOP.

Reading:

Learning to read has a logical sequence when taught well, however the wide range of texts that a child is exposed to as s/he learns to read, do not usually enable young children to develop confidence easily in those skills, within a progressive and logical system. Most schools use a range of reading schemes and 'real books' in order to allow pupils to consolidate their skills at a given level before moving on. Thus the range of vocabulary and structures the child is exposed to is not presented in a managed way. This renders the process of applying early skills daunting for many young children.

There is considerable evidence that raising attainment through 'Big Writing' and recycling of Basic Skills actually impacts on standards in reading, without teachers doing more about teaching reading than they have done previously.

The head teacher of Graveney Primary School in Kent (see Case Study 7) rang the writer in May 2005 because she was so excited about the dramatic rise in reading comprehensions levels across the school, as assessed through the use of the optional tests in May. Many pupils had risen 2 or more sub-levels since the implementation of Big Writing in late November 2004. Jane Troth attributes this progress primarily not only to pupils' improved understanding and use of extended language, but also to their capacity to write at length confidently and briskly, producing whole sentences and sections where previously they would have offered a word or line.

Text Types:

The National Strategies have given the teaching of text types a clear, logical structure with identified characteristics that can be modelled and analysed. However, the allocation of skills to specific text types has been a major flaw in the strategy, as most children do not believe they are allowed to use their full repertoires of words, phrases and structures, believing they belong only within the text type they were originally taught in.

'Big Writing' promotes rotating the writing across the range of text types on a weekly basis, thus covering the full range within a period of around eight weeks, while requiring evidence of use of the four generic targets (VCOP) in all text types (see Chapter 1.vii 'Changing the Text Types').

Spelling and Handwriting:

'Big Writing' promotes the ten minutes of Basic Skills each day to recycle all aspects of the Basic Skills. It also advises that all schools provide all staff (including Teaching Assistants) with annual refreshment on the school's method of teaching each of the basic skills, to ensure all are teaching in the same consistent way.

(See Chapter 8, 'The Importance of Basic Skills').

Writing Voice:
The process of learning to write and the development of pupils' 'voice and style' have not always been taught in an easily accessed, logical and sequential way before the introduction of Big Writing. Most teachers developed their own 'writing voice' through reading. They have a subconscious that enjoys language and so they unconsciously 'steal' words, phrases and structures, storing them for future use, as they consciously enjoy the content of the text.

This is the reason why most teachers fundamentally believe that to improve writing we must improve reading. The preferred method for improving the writing 'voice' for most teachers is to focus on the better understood process of reading comprehension, exposure of pupils to a range of texts, and the use of analysis to understand the characteristics of text and the construction of language (as advocated by the National Strategies). They believe that the children will then develop the 'writing voice' by a form of osmosis. (See Chapter 9 – What Really Does Raise Standards in Writing?)

4.iv   WHY ARE WE 'STEALING'?
The process is further complicated by the fact that most children do not 'own' language that they acquire from other texts.

In the same way that they currently believe the language and structures they are taught within the National Strategy's teaching of text types BELONGS to that text type and cannot be used elsewhere, many young children believe that language they learn through enjoyment of fiction, poetry etcetera belongs to the source material and cannot be used for any other purpose.

Even very young children can quote significant lines from traditional tales and nursery rhymes, but would never dream of using these in their own writing. Most young children know the following delightful constructions through their knowledge of early literature;

"Trip, trap, trip, trap...."

Could be applied to the arrival of a pony and rider in a piece of narrative writing e.g. 'Trip, trap, trip, trap, her pony's hooves rattled on the pathway'.

"Down came a woodpecker and...."

Could be applied to an eagle or a flying prehistoric monster swooping down e.g. 'Down came (swooped?) the enormous eagle and grabbed the.....'

"When the pie was opened...."

Could be applied to a treasure box or a special room e.g. 'When the heavy lid (or door) was opened, the....'

"There came a big spider...."

Could be applied to a monster or hero e.g. 'There came a hairy, green monster (or handsome, young prince)...'

In all these cases, the changing of the subject to the subject of a pupil's own writing would enhance the writing of any seven year old at the end of Key Stage 1. However, teachers do not usually find a child owning and adapting known traditional language in this way. Young children simply believe the learned phrases can only be used in a retell of the original source tale.

Big Writing is not in conflict with the National Strategies.

Big Writing is a teaching methodology that enables pupils to:

• Know explicitly what they have learned

• Own what they have learned

• Know explicitly that they MUST use what they have learned because that is what scores goals

• Use confidently what they have learned

• Transfer what they have learned confidently across genre and text type

• Know explicitly what they now need to do next

• Work confidently towards doing it

Teaching of VCOP is explicit teaching of the same skills as focusing on Grammar for Writing would achieve. The difference is that it has been synthesised into a form that enables clear, sequential teaching that is easily accessible and logical for children.

Mrs. Naylor, Year 6 teacher at Crossley Hall Primary School in Bradford, had one boy in Year 6 say to her, when introduced to VCOP,

"Why has no-one told us all this before?" (See also Chapter 7: 'The Difference Between Boys and Girls')

Janine Ryan, in her long study for her Master of Teaching degree (Case Study 4) quotes an average ability Year 6 pupil as saying,

"Now I actually know exactly how and with what to improve my writing. Before I knew it wasn't good, but apart from copying from books I was reading I didn't know what to do...."

Furthermore an above average ability pupil said,

"I feel like a teacher sometimes now because I can look at my friend's work and tell her what level she is working at in VCOP."

This clarity of structure and teaching, and the learning sequence for progression comes from the following aspects of Big Writing:

1. Teaching (through children discovering, 'stealing' and then owning the language by 'playing with' it) a vast range of ambitious vocabulary, connectives and openers, all at clearly identified levels of difficulty so that the child knows precisely what level he or she is selecting at, plus teaching the full range of punctuation from the Punctuation Pyramid, at least to Level 4, for all pupils.

2. Expecting pupils to 'own' the language through oral experimentation and demonstration, and through lively games and activities.

3. Teaching pupils explicitly what writing looks like at each level, and how they can use knowledge of VCOP, LDD and GHASP (Basic Skills) to identify the level of their own and others' writing. (See Chapter 8, 'The Importance of Basic Skills').

4. Making all pupils believe they are potentially Level 4/5 writers, and that the teacher will enable them to achieve this level.

5. Teaching pupils explicitly what the Big Writing Targets mean and how to use them, and showing children precisely what is wrong in their writing, therefore what they need to work on (and when to do it if a target is anything other than VCOP).

4.v   WHAT DOES EACH LEVEL LOOK LIKE?
Please note that the writer does not support the recommended practice of telling a pupil what sub-level he or she is working within.

This is positive for the pupil operating at or above the expected level, and may be motivational for a pupil slightly below the expected level. It often has, however, a negative impact on the attitudes of a pupil well below the expected level. Telling a pupil like Joshua (Case Study 2, Chapter 7 'The Difference Between Boys and Girls') that he is a Level 2c is likely to further disaffect him and CONFIRM his suspicion that he is failing as a writer and is 'no good' at it. Furthermore it makes the gap between his level of achievement and the expected

Level 4 seem insurmountable and therefore he is even less likely to try to bridge it.

The writer uses two strategies to motivate disaffected pupils:

1. Tell all pupils they are potentially high level writers (in Years 5 and 6 she tells all pupils they are Level 4/5 writers).

2. Teach all pupils explicitly what each level looks like, and what the different characteristics of the levels are, so that pupils can 'guestimate' the levels of given pieces. They will then be able to judge their current performance and know how to up-level it to the expected standard.

3. Teach all pupils to confidently identify use of VCOP in high level pieces, and give them ownership of those features, so that they are able to apply high level features in their own writing.

The writer uses regular samples of writing from her 'imaginary friend' to teach the levels (see Chapter 7, 'The Difference Between Boys and Girls') and pupils enjoy working in pairs or groups to up-level his work through insertion marks on paper copy, through word processing or through use of the interactive whiteboard.

This then extends to receiving back their own writing and up-levelling it together in similar ways.

The increasing confidence and speed achieved within this process soon enables pupils to up-level using omission marks when given the 'five minute' warning at the end of Big Writing or a writing assessment/test.

34 CHAPTER 5:
THE PROCESS OF TARGET SETTING IN BIG WRITING

 Chapter 5 explores issues around target setting and the importance of small-step targets for pupils' success. It also provides a model for child-centred small-step targets in writing.

5.i WHAT IS THE CRITERION SCALE AND HOW DO WE USE IT TO SET TARGETS?

The Criterion Scale is an accurate tool for assessing all writing, regardless of text type or genre. It gives reliable judgements within all levels and sub-levels from Working Towards Level 1 (W1) to Level 5.

Use of the Criterion Scale to assess writing and to set personal targets for pupils is explained in both previous publications ('Raising Standards in Writing' and 'Strategies for Immediate Impact on Writing Standards').

The Criterion Scale and all other Big Writing resources are now available on CD Rom through the website, www.twentytwentyvision.org.uk.

When the teacher uses the Criterion Scale to assess a pupil's writing, s/he ticks if a pupil has shown secure evidence of a skill, puts a dot if there is a suggestion of evidence but not enough for a secure judgement, and puts a cross if there is no evidence at all.

The teacher counts the ticks and uses the threshold boxes in the Criterion Scale to decide the sub-level the pupil is performing at. If the judgement is on a threshold between two sub-levels, always move the judgement downwards and allocate the lower level, as pupils on a threshold move backwards and forwards between the two sub-levels until skills are consolidated, or in their own response to the stimulus, the text type or their mood.

Immediate impact targets are informed by two sorts of judgements:

• skills that are clearly long overdue for a pupil writing at that level, e.g. the pupil may have very good 'voice and style' but may not be using full stops and capital letters to show sentences, or may be writing at a high level yet handwriting is immature

•skills where there are indicators of the pupil beginning to use them (dots), and which, with a small 'push', could be quickly in place

Now identify the pupil's current skill level within the hierarchy for the aspect of GHASP or VCOP that the immediate impact targets are part of, and that will inform of the next small step required (see below and Chapter 5.v, 'Child Friendly Small Step Targets for Big Writing).

5.ii HOW MANY TARGETS SHOULD WE SET?

Identify three targets only.

More than three targets is daunting. Less may restrict progress, as the teacher should work on the theory that given three a pupil may struggle with one, but will still get two. At most sub-levels gaining three more ticks can often be sufficient to move a pupil up another sub-level, if s/he was already secure within the level. If s/he was on the threshold gaining three more criteria will make the pupil's level secure.

If a pupil has weaknesses in basic skills, either one or two of the small step targets should focus on this aspect. At least one target should always be from VCOP for all pupils at Level 2B or above.

Now move to the target boxes for each aspect, (see 5.v 'Child Friendly Small Step Targets for Big Writing') and compare the targets with the pupil's current skill level as exhibited in the piece of assessed writing. Set the next step target as the small step for the pupil, unless a smaller, intermediate step can be identified.

Explain the meaning of all targets to the class or group as a whole. Point out that:

• If their target is about progression within VCOP it will be achieved routinely through 'playing' the VCOP games and then using the skills in writing.

• If it is GHASP (Basic Skills) or VCOP that the pupil should already have known (e.g. use of full stop/capital letter to show sentences or use of adjectives and adverbs for a pupil otherwise writing at 2a or above) the teacher will show the pupil exactly what needs to be done. It can then be addressed by the pupil both during the process of writing, and through going back and inserting throughout their writing when given the 'five minute' warning at the end of Big Writing. (See below in Chapter 5.iii 'How and When Do We Address Their 'Past their Sell-by Date' Targets?')

5.iii HOW AND WHEN DO WE ADDRESS 'PAST THEIR SELL-BY DATE TARGETS?'

All pupils who have one 'past their sell-by date' target are told that for the next five weeks, when the teacher says, 'You have five minutes left' in the writing part of Big Writing, the child's priority is not to finish his/her writing, but rather to stop, go back and correct the target throughout the piece.

If this is done for 5 weeks, the child will begin to self-correct as s/he writes.

The teacher acknowledges this progress and achievement through weekly marking, praising as progress is made and, when the error is consistently addressed, she or he sets the next step target in the aspect, using the Target Box for information. When the skill is consistently addressed at the appropriate level for the child's age and writing level, or when it is fully accurate, the teacher monitors for maintenance and sets a new basic skill target or, if all Basic Skills are now accurate, switches to all VCOP targets.

Thus the pupil has known explicitly what he or she must do in the last five minutes of Big Writing time in order to achieve the small step and move forward.

✚ The following are examples of small step targets that might be given as 'past their sell-by date' targets to be addressed in the last five minutes:

• Can I pull all the tails in my writing below the line?

• Can I put in full stops?

• Can I put capital letters after every full stop?

• Can I get rid of capital letters that are in the wrong places?

• Can I open sentences in different ways?

• Can I use connectives to extend sentences?

Up to Level 2c all targets may focus on the following aspects:

• Handwriting

• Spelling – sight words and phonics

• Sentence structure/basic punctuation

• Legibility

• Increased length

• Sequence words to open sentences

• First connectives for extension

From Level 2b upwards at least one of the three targets should be from VCOP, often two will be and sometimes all three will be VCOP, usually when all Basic Skills are secure.

Although two targets may be from Basic Skills from Level 2b upwards, only one should be given as a quick impact 'past their sell-by date' target for work in the last 5 minutes. Therefore a more able and/or older pupil may be given two small steps in one. For example:

• Can I use full stops and capital letters to show sentence structure?
• Can I use ascenders and descenders (sticks and tails) correctly?
• Can I use spelling correctly, both sight words and phonics?

5.iv   LENGTH, DETAIL AND DESCRIPTION (LDD)
This aspect is addressed through the 'Story Structure'

cards introduced in 'Strategies for Immediate Impact on Writing Standards'. In that publication teachers were advised to make attractive, laminated, coloured A4 cards with the following captions.

COLOUR 1	STORY STRUCTURE CARDS	OPENING BODY ENDING
COLOUR 2	KEY WORDS CARDS	WHO WHAT WHERE WHEN HOW (3 of each)
COLOUR 3	DESCRIPTION CARDS	May simply say, 'DESCRIBE' May define e.g. 'APPEARANCE' OR 'FEELINGS' (3 of each)

The cards are then used several times as a kinaesthetic process of building story structure. The following is the process for the kinaesthetic process:

1. Children holding the three structure cards (1.) stand as far apart as possible, holding up their card. They should be in the correct sequence for a story. Usually the three children are asked to 'write' a story without speaking. It can take them a few minutes to work out that they should stand in the correct sequence, and occasionally the class are asked to help by advising them. They will always stand close together. The teacher then asks them to 'write a longer story' and eventually children work out that they should spread out. Now the teacher can point out that when we want to write a longer story there is a lot of space that needs to be filled up. This is the job of the 5 key words; who, what, where, when and how.

2. Next, any children with the 5 key word cards (2.) identify where they might stand in the story and say what sort of character, setting, time etcetera they might be. e.g. The 'who' in the opening may be the main character. The 'who' in the body may be the villain and the 'who' in the ending may be the hero. The class is told that in each section of the writing they should write about at least 3 of the 5 key words, and should stop to describe at least one. Because of the number of key word cards distributed, there will often be one of each key word in each section of this model.

3. Finally, children who are holding description cards (3.) stand behind chosen key card holders, holding the word 'description' above the head of the holder of the key card. They say how that aspect might be described, and why.Children can be asked to move to another position in the line and say how their role might now have changed. For example, "Mrs. Who, if you moved to the body of the story what sort of character might you be now?"

Children can be asked to make up a simple story by each child in turn making up a phrase or sentence that represents their card, as in 'Consequences'. This will need support in the early stages but can be great fun and often quite amusing. Many pupils can learn to give unlikely or challenging cues for the next person.

Example of Consequences for Story Structure:

1. Pupil with OPENING card: 'It was early in the morning...'

2. Pupil with WHEN card: 'A long time ago....'

3. Pupil with WHO card: 'A very old woman....'

4. Pupil with WHERE card: 'Came out of the forest...'

5. Pupil with HOW card: 'Walking very slowly...'

6. Pupil with WHAT card: 'Gathering sticks for her fire.'

Now a DESCRIPTION card is held above the pupils could describe the weather or something relevant to the time, for example;

"It was the moment of first bird song, early in the morning..."

When all pupils are confident at playing consequences, the cards are displayed in a line at the top of one wall in the classroom, for example there is often available space above the windows.

• The OPENING card is placed at the left hand end of the space, with WHO, WHAT, WHERE, WHEN, HOW clustered round it and the DESCRIPTION WORD/S to left and right.

• The BODY card is placed in the middle, with WHO, WHAT, WHERE, WHEN, HOW clustered round it and the DESCRIPTION WORD/S to left and right.

• The ENDING card is placed at the right hand end of the space, with WHO, WHAT, WHERE, WHEN, HOW clustered round it and the DESCRIPTION WORD/S to left and right.

Pupils are given three 'goals' before they start to write. These may be three grapes, slices of tangerine or slices of apple.

They are told:

1. When you think you have finished the opening look up there. Have you written about at least three (key words) and have you stopped and described at least one? Then you have finished the opening. Eat a goal and move down.

2. When you think you have finished the body look up there. Have you written about at least three (key words) and have you stopped and described at least one? Then you have finished the body. Eat a goal and move down.

3. When you think you have finished the ending look up there. Have you written about at least three (key words) and have you stopped and described at least one? Then you have finished the ending. Eat a goal and go back an up-level using insertion marks (upside down v).

THIS PROCESS ALSO TEACHES PARAGRAPHING SKILLS QUICKLY AND EASILY TO CHILDREN AS YOUNG AS SIX.

5.v   CHILD FRIENDLY SMALL STEP TARGETS FOR BIG WRITING
(See also Chapter 8.iii 'Small Step Targets')

The following targets can be given to pupils with the language modified as appropriate.

They should be explained clearly to the whole class, and re-explained to individual pupils upon first receipt, if it is felt the pupil might need further help.

The numbers indicate the National Curriculum (NC) Level of the skill.

The Roman numerals indicate more than one target within an NC level, e.g. 1 i and 1 ii means two separate targets within Level 1.

The small letters indicate NC sub-levels, e.g. L2c means the lowest of the three sub-levels within Level 2.

 NB If a pupil would benefit from one of the targets below being broken down into even smaller steps through making it the learning of one specific piece of punctuation, letter, word or group of words, this should be done.

✛ TARGETS FOR PUNCTUATION

1. i Can you point to full stops followed by capital letters in other people's writing? (oral target at WL1 and L1)

ii. Can you try to use full stops and capital letters to show where sentences begin and end?

2. i Can you use full stops and capital letters to show sentences?

ii. Can you always use full stops and capital letters accurately to show sentences?

iii. Can you use question marks?

3. i Can you use level 3 range of punctuation (. ! ? ,) usually accurately?

ii. Can you begin to use punctuation for effect (! ....)?

iii. Can you experiment with Level 4 and 5 punctuation?

4. Can you use Level 4 range of punctuation, usually accurately? (May be initially given one at a time)

5. i Can you use the full range of punctuation, usually accurately? (May be initially given Level 5 specifics one at a time)

ii. Can you use the full range of punctuation accurately?

🖈 **NB** The above can be reduced to even smaller steps through giving each piece of punctuation one at a time, however many pupils can handle experimentation with a whole level at once at least up to Level 4.

✛ TARGETS FOR OPENERS AND CONNECTIVES

1. Can you use 'and' to join simple sentences?

2. i Can you use simple linking words and phrases? (e.g. Last time, also, after, then, soon, at last etc)

ii. Can you use simple sequence words? (E.g. First, then, next, last, before, after, etc)

iii. Can you use a wider range of connectives,(e.g. but, so, then if, or, because, when?)

3. i Can you use Level 3 connectives (when, if, because, after) including as openers sometimes? (Could be reduced to 5 separate targets, one for each of the connectives and then one to sometimes use them as openers).

ii. Can you use Level 3 linking and sequence words? (Afterwards, before, also, after a while etc.) (Could be reduced to separate targets, one for each or pairs of targeted words).

iii. Can you use 'ly' and 'ing' words to open? (Could be given one at a time)

4. i Can you use Level 4 connectives and often as openers? (Although, however, as well as, since, as a result of etc.)

ii. Can you use Level 4 links and sequence phrases? (Eventually, as a result of, because of etc.)

iii. Can you use Level 4 'ly' and 'ing' words?

5. i Can you use sophisticated openers and connectives? (In addition to, As if, never the less, despite, contrary to etc.)

ii. Can you use sophisticated linking and sequence words and phrases? (Previously, initially, consequently, additionally, undoubtedly, subsequently etc.)

Targets for Ambitious Vocabulary

1. i. Can you use simple adjectives and adverbs to describe?

ii. Can you use some ambitious words ('wow' words)?

2. i. Can you use a range of ambitious vocabulary?

ii. Can you try to use generalising words (e.g. sometimes, never, often, always)?

3. i. Can you use a wide range of ambitious vocabulary?

ii. Can you use a wider range of generalising words (e.g. all at L3 plus others such as: sometimes, never, often, usually, always, suddenly, just, about, (as in 'about five') around, (as in 'around five') etc.)?

4. i. Can you use a wide range of ambitious vocabulary accurately and selected precisely for purpose?

ii. Can you use a wide range of generalising words (e.g. all at L3 and L4 plus others such as: about to, every LAST bit, but STILL, of course, maybe, perhaps, possibly, could be, etc.)

5. Can you use literary effects such as onomatopoeia, alliteration, metaphor and simile?

Targets for Handwriting

W1. i. Can you recognise and try to draw all letter shapes (can be differentiated into smaller steps by clustering small groups of like letters together.)?

ii. Can you start letters in the correct place? (can be differentiated into smaller steps by addressing singly or clustering small groups of similar together)?

iii. Do you know writing goes from left to right in English?

iv. Can you attempt to write from left to right?

v. Can you write your own name (see also 'Spelling')?

1. i. Can you draw letters the right size and shape?

ii. Can you use capital and small letters (upper/lower case) and sticks and tails (ascenders/descenders) correctly?

2c. Can you do neat, regular writing?

2b. Can you use neat, accurate writing with some evidence of joining?

2a. Can you use neat, joined writing (may be a little irregular)?

3. i. Can you usually use neat, accurate, joined writing (may be a little slow)?

ii. Can you usually use neat, accurate, joined writing with flow?

4. i. Can you always write neatly and accurately?

ii. Can you adapt handwriting for purpose?

Targets for Spelling

W1.i. Can you pick out your own name from others (oral)?

ii. Can you try to write your own name (may be first letter only at first)?

iii. Can you write your own name (letter size and shape may be irregular)?

iv. Can you copy/trace words and try to write a few on your own?

1. i. Can you read sight words from Reception and Year 1 NLS word lists (Teach in small groups of like letters)?

ii. Can you use letter sounds to read and write – CVC words spelt correctly (Teach in small groups of like words)?

iii. Can you try to spell sight words from Reception and Year 1 word lists (teach in small groups of like words)?

2c. i. Can you usually spell common (single syllable) words correctly?

ii. Can you use simple phonics well enough that most words can be read or decoded?

2b.i. Can you spell all common (single syllable) words correctly?

ii. Can you use a wider range of phonic strategies?

2a.i. Can you spell most common polysyllabic words (more than one syllable) correctly? (E.g. today, bonfire, having, keeper)?

ii. Can you spell all sight words from KS1 accurately?

3. i. Can you spell a wider range of sight words (includes appropriate KS2 NLS lists)?

ii. Can you use a range of strategies for longer or more complex unknown words?

4. i. Can you spell a wide range of known sight words (includes majority of all the NLS Key Stage 1 and 2 lists)?

ii. Can you use good strategies for all unknown words, confidently?

5. Can you spell both common and ambitious words, almost always accurately?

Targets for Length, Detail and Description, (LDD)

W1.i. Can you try to write simple sentences, labels, titles or other text?

ii. Can you copy someone else's writing?

1.i. Can you write your own ideas so that others can read and understand them?

2c Can you write several sentences (or more) about one idea? Some sentences should be joined by connectives such as 'and', or 'but' and 'so'.

2b/ai. Can you write a longer piece with extended sentences?

ii. Can you use adjectives, adverbs and descriptive phrases to add detail?

iii. Can you write about at least 3 of the 5 key elements (who, what, how, when, why)?

3.i. Can you write a longer piece with an opening, a body and an ending, each of which has at least of the 3 key elements (w.w.w.w.h.) and where you have stopped and described at least one?

ii. Is your writing usually lively and interesting with LDD?

4.i. Can you use paragraphs accurately?

ii. Is your writing always lively and interesting with good LDD?

iii. Are you beginning to use a good range of organisational devices?

5. Is your writing always well organised, using a wide range of organisational and literary devices accurately?

**"Today is Big Writing Day.
I love it 'cos no-ones away!
You can jump up the levels
Like hungry young devils
And when the candle is blown
There is one long groan,
It's the end of Big Writing Day!"**

Isiah and Shane
Year 6, Crossley Hall Primary School, Bradford.

42 CHAPTER 6:
METHODS AND MOTIVATORS

 Chapter 6 explores issues around when and why we often need to use motivators in the short term, and ways in which teaching methods can affect motivation. It includes a model for 'Teaching Through Talk' (The Triple T Method) that motivates all children and ensures Assessment for Learning.

6.i   BACKGROUND

Most children start school as lively, energetic and enthusiastic three to four year olds, with huge self-belief about their capacity to 'do' anything. Yet by the age of nine some of these beliefs and attitudes have become modified and even lost in the classroom for a significant number of children. (See Chapter 7.iii 'The Importance of Recycling') Many children in our schools believe there are some things they are 'no good' at.

What can we do about it?

Teaching should be fast, lively and fun!

Teachers must bring enthusiasm and passion back into their teaching. The last fifteen years have seen creativity and excitement driven out of many classrooms through the volume of the National Curriculum, the National Strategies and the pressures of OFSTED, national tests and published national league tables.

This Chapter discusses the contributions as methods and motivators of:

- expectations,
- awareness of concentration spans,
- Assessment for Learning,
- teaching through talk,
- the creative curriculum,
- incentives and rewards,
- ethos.

It also references a curriculum model that would enrich teaching.

If teaching is to be brisk and lively, teachers must be confident in their subject knowledge and passionate about children's learning. They must also BELIEVE that every child can succeed.

6.ii   'EXPECTATIONS SHAPE OUTCOMES!'

If a teacher is working in a school where s/he does not believe eighty-five percent or more of children can achieve the expected Level 4 or above in the core subjects of English, mathematics and science, then he or she should move on.

In schools where adults blame the community and/or the homes for pupils' low achievement, the adults are suffering from low expectations. The reality is that a few schools can 'get away with' satisfactory to good teaching when the aspirations and cultural experiences of homes and community compensate. However, teaching must usually be very good or excellent when the majority of children have limited access to language, discussion, literature and enriched life experiences outside the school.

Low expectations communicate themselves to pupils. A pupil's self belief is influenced by the expectations of the adults around him/her and in their belief in his/her ability to succeed.

"If you think you can or you think you can't, you're probably right." (Henry Ford)

The writer herself used to say, 'Who says eighty percent of pupils can get Level 4?' Now she firmly believes the current national target of 85% can be achieved, and knows she will see it in schools where 'Big Writing' has been adopted and is being systematically and enthusiastically taught.

What Can We Do About It?

We must all challenge low expectations when we meet them. Talented teachers are proving that children in the most unfortunate circumstances and those whose lives are frequently in crisis can achieve as well as more privileged and secure peers. Senior Managers need to celebrate the achievements that are evident in some classrooms and initiate debate on why similar achievements are not occurring in all classrooms.

6.iii   THE IMPACT OF WHAT WE KNOW ABOUT CONCENTRATION SPANS

Teaching must reflect what we know about children's capacity to maintain concentration. Research shows that most children can only concentrate for the number of minutes equivalent to the number of years they have been alive, plus one. Therefore a 5 year old can only concentrate for 6 minutes and a 10 year old for 11 minutes.

If we do not provide children with brain breaks at appropriate intervals, they will take them anyway. They lose concentration, and when they refocus on what we are saying they have missed a significant part and often cannot re-access the learning. They may then lose concentration altogether because it is not coherent for them.

What Can We Do About it?

We should never focus on one aspect of input or activity for more than ten minutes without giving pupils a 'brain break' or opportunity to refocus. This might be through strategies such as use of a short discussion, telling a partner what they have just learned, or a series of mini-plenaries. (See 'A Structure for Teaching that Ensures Assessment for Learning' below).

When teaching is brisk, however, it is all the more important to recycle and provide at least three opportunities for children to access the learning. The Assessment for Learning model that follows, ensures recycling of key objectives, giving all pupils opportunity to embed the learning. Teachers should also remember that it is only when children can use and apply newfound knowledge and skills in a range of diverse situations that we can be sure that the learning has taken place.

6.iv 'A STRUCTURE FOR TEACHING THAT ENSURES ASSESSMENT FOR LEARNING'

The following is a model for the use of objectives that supports children's access to new learning, and teachers' use of formative assessment skills to confirm learning. It may be deployed in any subject or lesson.

The quality of teaching is now judged by the quality of learning in the classroom. Teachers need to refine their teaching so that they are able to judge, with certainty, what the pupils have learned and understood.

This model builds on the best practice for Assessment for Learning (A for L).

**TEACHING THROUGH TALK
(The 'Triple T' Method for A for L)**

The following model is appropriate for teaching in all subjects and with all ages.

The Triple Talk Method for A for L has 4 main stages (at least 3 of them must involve talk):

- Pupil talk during and after the taught input (if longer than ten minutes)

- Pupil talk after the explanation of the activity

- Pupils talk in mini plenaries during the activity if longer than 10 minutes

- Pupil talk during the final plenary

At every stage pupils are expected to be able to state simply and clearly what they have learned, and from Stage 2, how it is to be or may be used.

The Process for the 'Triple T Method':

1) Share the Key Objectives with pupils:
- What are we going to do?
- Why are we doing it?

2) Teach the knowledge and skills:
- Model/demonstrate and question

📌 **NB** If Step 2 is to take longer than 10 minutes it should be punctuated by mini breaks through pupils talking in pairs in response to adult questions e.g., 'Tell each other what you have just learned please', 'Why do you think it might be like that?' 'How might we have used this when we were doing X last week?' 'Who do you think is going to need to know about this?' 'What do you think you still need to know in order to use this?' etc.

3) Tell pupils to talk to their partners:
- What have you learned?
- How is it used?

Did they all know? If not:
- Confident child re-explains to the class.

4) Explain the activity:
- What are we going to do?
- Why we are doing it?
- Model the process.

5) Talk to your partner:
- What have you to do?
- Why are you doing it?

Did they all know? If not:
- Confident child re-explains to the class.

6) Give children a 'job' while moving to/preparing for activity? e.g.
- Count backwards from......
- Times Table
- Discuss X
- Be planning Y (OPTIONAL)

7) Monitor as all begin work. Do all look confident? Challenged? (At both levels = challenged and therefore excited/challenged as in can't do?)

8) Support generally or work with a group but ensure you can see/monitor the whole classroom from your base point.

9) Mini-plenary every 10 minutes as they work (at maximum to UKS2, then may be 15 minutes in longer sessions)
- What are we doing?
- Why are we doing it?
- Here's a good example so far...... OR
- How will we know if we have been successful? OR
- Is this one going to be successful? How do you know? OR
- I heard this interesting comment ....
- What does it suggest? OR
  Has anyone...............? etc

10) Final Plenary:
- What did we learn?
- How did we use it?
- Here are good examples. How do we KNOW they are good?
- What if I had asked you to X instead? How would the outcome have been different? (Transferring the learning. It is only when pupils can transfer what they have learned that we KNOW learning has taken place.)
- Next lesson we will do that and see how it is different, OR
- We shall be moving on to.....

Teachers may wish to exemplify the Triple T Method (A for L) in every lesson they teach, ensuring that children's learning is evident and quantifiable. This will particularly help to confirm that all pupils are in control of their learning and understand how to demonstrate what has been learned.

This model promotes the use of talk to enable assessment of pupils' learning, and ensures that everyone, including pupils themselves, knows explicitly what each child has learned.

EVERY PUPIL SHOULD BE ABLE TO STATE CLEARLY BUT BRIEFLY AT THE END OF EVERY LESSON, WHAT THEY HAVE LEARNED AND HOW IT WAS USED.

If they can't, how do we know they have learned it?

Pupils should also be involved in the setting of their own targets. Many teachers struggle to identify specific 'small step' targets to enable pupils to build sequentially onto prior learning. Big Writing provides an excellent vehicle for target setting and pupils are enabled to verbalise explicitly what they need to do to move towards the next level of achievement.
(See Chapter 4 'What is Effective Target Setting')

6.v   TEACHING THROUGH TALK (General)

Talk has been identified as one of the preferred learning styles for boys. Promoting learning through talk motivates many boys, and what is good for the boys is good for the girls. (See Chapter 7, 'The Difference Between Boys and Girls').

Teachers should actively promote talk in the classroom and, for bilingual pupils in homes where English is not the first language of daily use, children should be expected to translate all their learning into first language so that they can share it with family at home and give parents the opportunity to support them in making appropriate cultural and experiential links.

It is not enough to PERMIT both talk and 'code switching' (moving between English and first language) teachers should expect and REQUIRE it.
H.M.C.I. David Bell observed that there is too much teacher talk and not enough pupil talk in the classroom. Effective schools may wish to take the implications of this on board.

Living in poverty is one of the most significant factors in underachievement and low standards. This is especially true in writing. Poverty is frequently associated with stress for adults, and stress can lead to restricted communication with children. Even adults who in other circumstances would be highly articulate, may lapse into restricted code due to the strain of living in poverty. Poverty is often (although not always) associated with language deprivation and many children who live in poverty grow up with a restricted code of speech. They may have rich and expressive 'street language' appropriate to their communities, but few or no higher

order language structures to support writing at secure Level 4 and Level 5.

One of the key contributions of the Early Years' setting in raising standards in writing is the development of pupils' language skills. (See Chapter 3, 'The Contribution of the Foundation Stage). If children enter Year 1 able to talk confidently in extended sentences and are developing a rich and varied vocabulary, then their early educational experiences have given them a great gift towards becoming a writer.

6.vi   THE CREATIVE CURRICULUM

Nobody who was in the profession in the 1970s and 1980s would deny, in hindsight, that there was often a lack of rigour in the curriculum. The writer remembers transferring between schools in two different Local Education Authorities in January 1990, and telephoning several times prior to the move to request the medium term planning for the next term, having been advised that the 'topic' was 'Canals'. Eventually the information came back in a telephone message, 'Basically we work through the Ladybird Book, doing a page a week.'

The National Curriculum has brought improved subject knowledge across the ten subjects it covers. However, it has consistently remained overloaded, despite two major rewrites and the provision of detailed Schemes of Work from the Qualifications and Curriculum Association (QCA).

Indeed, the QCA Schemes have replaced the National Curriculum, (NC) as the dictate of teaching for many teachers, who have sometimes been heard to say, 'We can't do that, it isn't in the QCA.' In actual fact most QCA Schemes are too overloaded to be taught in their entirety, and this has led to teachers playing at 'pick and mix', taking the bits they like from a Unit and leaving the rest. This can lead to fragmentation, and some aspects that are actually key elements of the NC Programmes of Study, which are the actual legal requirement of the National Curriculum, being neglected. The QCA Units often create a confusing assessment picture due to conflicting assessment foci in the units, which sometimes have not only lesson objectives, but also learning outcomes and End of Unit expectations that do not complement one another.

The rapid pace required to cover as much as possible of an overloaded curriculum has been a deterrent to developing investigative approaches, enquiry learning and the use of extended discussion. It has encouraged many teachers to depend on direct delivery of content through limited resources and instructional input.

Some teachers are afraid to make bold decisions in reshaping the curriculum, and some Head Teachers actually discourage significant change, despite the permission implicit in 'Excellence and Enjoyment', the

Department for Education and Skills, (DfES) publication of 2003.

The above publication states that it wants schools feel they have the freedom to:

 'Take a fresh look at their curriculum, their timetable and the organisation of the school day and week, and think actively about how they would like to develop and enrich the experience they offer their children.'
('Excellence and Enjoyment' 2003, Page 12)

Teachers can sometimes be resistant to major curricular change because it means changing their planning and often taking on board new subject knowledge. The writer maintains that without significant curricular change it is unlikely that teachers will re-invigorate their teaching and bring excitement back into the classroom.

'Excellence and Enjoyment' states that;

 'Children learn better when they are excited and engaged – but what excites them best is truly excellent teaching, which challenges them and shows them what they can do.' (Foreword)

'The Creative Curriculum' (Ros. Wilson, pending, Autumn 2006) provides a curriculum model that enables teachers to identify clear links across subjects. This supports teachers in designing learning opportunities that bring the skills and knowledge of more than one subject area together.

'The Creative Curriculum' has been planned predominantly from the QCA Schemes of Work, but with massive reduction. This encourages a teacher to refer back to the referenced Scheme for further subject knowledge or ideas for activities if s/he is unclear about an aspect. The medium term 'Creative Curriculum Maps' enable teachers to see curricular links at a glance and thus to use the key questions (medium term objectives) to inform their short term planning.

There are more opportunities for the foundation subjects planned than teachers are required to deliver (especially for history and geography) and thus this enables further choice for the teachers and Senior Managers of a school, prioritising according to the needs of their pupils and the opportunities available in the community in order to personalise the curriculum.

Furthermore, this curriculum enables teachers to plan 'challenges' that move the learning into creative short term opportunities for investigative and skill-based learning. Examples of short term Creative Curriculum Challenges and Mini Challenges are provided. It is also planned to be assessed through a hierarchy of generic

learning skills synthesized out of the Level Descriptions for every single subject of the National Curriculum. This hierarchy is included in the publication.

6.vii INCENTIVES AND REWARDS

Pupils who have become disaffected with regard to a subject, or an aspect of a subject (as many boys and some girls have towards writing), have developed deep seated attitudes towards the issue that may be difficult to change. These have usually been formed through negative self-belief, the pupil believes he/she is 'no good' at it and thus does not enjoy doing it and may even avoid it. (See Chapter 7, 'The Difference Between Boys and Girls').

High quality teaching that includes frequent praise and positive reinforcement will help to combat these attitudes and lead to revised self-belief for a pupil. However, this can be a long process, particularly for a pupil with low self-esteem and/or coping with other stress factors in her/his life. Telling a child that he has great potential and that if he tries hard at this new aspect of learning he will succeed, is not always immediately effective for a child who believes he has tried hard in the past and has not made progress. He now believes he 'will never be any good at it'!

Incentives and rewards produce quick gains for these pupils.

Everyone subscribes to the theory that success and achievement should be reward enough, however, the reality is that many teachers are working with pupils with deep seated antipathy to an aspect of learning and a legacy of long term failure and lack of self-belief. Schools are also working under great pressure to make rapid changes in standards. Sometimes we have to sacrifice principles in the short term for greater good in the long term.

Promising quick gratification encourages a disaffected pupil to 'have a go' purely to 'win' the reward, even though he or she does not necessarily believe he/she will get any better. If the target he/she is asked to have a go at is an appropriately small and achievable step that will show quick success (as are the steps in 'Big Writing') the pupil finds to his amazement that he not only 'wins' the reward but that he also makes measurable progress.

Very quickly the incentives and rewards may be 'forgotten' as the more desirable motivators of progress and achievement take over. (See also, Chapter 1, 'What is 'Big Writing').

Schools revising their curriculum need to identify the core skills needed for high achievement and plan to teach and consolidate these through a range of different and exciting learning opportunities.

6.viii THE IMPORTANCE OF ETHOS

The importance of ethos cannot be too highly emphasised.

Pupils should live and work in a learning culture that is based on mutual respect between pupils and adults, courtesy, praise, positive reinforcement and the celebration of achievement for all.

The whole premise of 'Big Writing' is about these qualities, and if pupils are not enjoying Big Writing then it is not likely that the method is being implemented in the recommended way.

Furthermore, the environmental changes recommended for the second session (see Chapter 1, 'What is Big Writing') contribute to a spiritual atmosphere that has been recognised and reported in OFSTED reports (see Case Studies 3,9 and 10, excerpts from the Heaton Primary School, New Hall J.I.N.C. School and Wilsden Primary School OFSTED reports.)

**"Half way through the week
Is Big Writing,
A subject we all find inviting,
We use V.C.O.P.
That's THE key for me!
Connectives and openers uniting!"**

Kyle and Hasmita
Year 5, Crossley Hall Primary School, Bradford.

48 CHAPTER 7:
THE DIFFERENCE BETWEEN BOYS AND GIRLS

 This chapter examines issues around the gap in achievement between boys and girls in writing and makes suggestions for addressing this. It includes the second of our Case Studies, Joshua Fieldhouse.

THE DIFFERENCE BETWEEN BOYS AND GIRLS

This publication is not a research paper. It does not, therefore, reference the wealth of publications on brain based learning, learning styles and boys' achievement that has informed the writer's work in education. It is important, however, to acknowledge the role of the publications from the Network Press in this work, and also the impact of 'How to Raise Boys' Achievement' by Noble, Brown and Murphy, (Fulton 2002).

7.i   MAKING CONNECTIONS:

Those familiar with brain based learning will be aware that for many boys the connections between the two hemispheres of the brain are not as pronounced as they are for most girls. This has been found to render some boys less likely to make spontaneous links and connections with prior learning, or with experiences in other subjects or areas of learning. It is, therefore, crucial that teachers make the links and connections explicit for all pupils, and clearly all will benefit from this.

WHAT CAN WE DO ABOUT IT?

It would be helpful for each teacher to receive an excellent example of the exercise books completed for each subject in the previous year of education. Then, as learning that builds on progressively is commenced, pupils can be reminded of where and when they met it before, showing the work they undertook as a visual hook to enable the connections to be made.

Hooks are planned strategies that enable pupils to make links to previous learning or to recall and access previous learning. Examples of effective hooks are:

- Visual prompts such as seeing a previously used visual aid or work completed, use of the same resource or scaffold, or use of a trigger visual such as a title, caption, colour, logo, character, font or emblem that, having been explicitly explained, represents the learning.

- Oral/aural prompts such as slogans, captions, chants, learned phrases, a significant piece of music, chorus or musical phrase or a song (see Case Study 10, Wilsden Primary School)

- Kinaesthetic prompts such as a particular brain gym activity, arm, hand or finger action.

As teachers prepare the introduction to each new unit of study, therefore, they have key responsibilities that will enhance the learning experience for all pupils, and especially boys:

1. Tell pupils what they are going to learn within the unit, (content knowledge), and publish on the classroom wall or a flip chart page that can be referred to weekly.

2. Tell the pupils which key skills they are going to develop or further develop, and publish on the classroom wall or a flip chart page that can be protected and referred to weekly.

3. Make explicit the connections between this unit and prior learning experiences within the same subject, preferably showing a visual hook and providing time for pupils to remember the previous learning through talk.

4. Make explicit the connections between the learning they are to experience and similar learning, both content and skills, in other subjects, both in the past and being taught in parallel through other subjects and areas of study this term, showing visual hooks when appropriate.

5. Make explicit how they are going to use the skills, and what success will look like.

All the above must then be referred to regularly, whenever opportunity for making the connections arises. In addition, use brain gym to enhance connections between the hemispheres of the brain (see Network Press publications).

7.ii   STARTING SCHOOLING

Research shows that we begin academic education in a school setting in England at too young an age for the majority of boys. In some countries in Europe, for example Finland, where children start formal schooling at age six, boys of primary age more often achieve similarly to girls.

One of the significant differences between boys and girls is that, in general, girls in primary schools want to please the adults around them. If they get something wrong, girls up to the age of twelve will usually work harder the next time to get it right, because they like the feel-good factor of being praised and being successful. Most boys, on the other hand, do not like to fail and, if they feel failure is likely, they often avoid the situation.

Because many boys (and some girls) are meeting the writing experience before the age at which they are ready for it, they do not always experience early success as writers in the Foundation Stage and as a consequence do not enjoy early writing experiences. Although professionals around young children avoid making comparisons between the achievements of different children, family members and friends are often less generous, not realising the harm that may be done to the child's self-belief, and at some point the child is often made aware that he/she is not succeeding as well as others at writing. Eventually, even the individual himself is able to recognise the difference between his own mark making and the emergent writing of others around him.

Research shows us that self-belief is often the single most influential factor in whether a child achieves at his/her optimum potential, and that it is not necessarily the explicit messages a child receives that form his self-belief, but the ongoing peripheral and hidden messages. A boy who believes he is good at writing will usually do well at it, but a boy who believes he is 'no good' will often avoid the writing activity and may become disaffected towards writing.

'IF YOU THINK YOU CAN OR YOU THINK YOU CAN'T YOU ARE PROBABLY RIGHT!'
(Henry Ford)

As soon as a boy in the Foundation Stage setting or Key Stage 1 gets the message that he is doing less well than others his age at writing, he begins to believe he is 'no good' at it and he will often avoid the mark making/writing opportunities. This results in him dropping even further behind. As he moves through Key Stage 1, where the writing activities are usually whole class time-tabled opportunities and thus are less avoidable, a child may now find he is significantly behind most girls and some boys. He has now begun the journey towards being a disaffected writer, and he will write the bare minimum that he feels he can get away with.

We live and work in a country where pupils and schools are measured and compared at age seven, and thus great importance is placed on starting children on the writing journey as early as possible, even though Foundation Stage practitioners are aware that many boys and some girls are not yet ready for this type of learning. Thus a significant number of boys and some girls are placed in a failing situation, and they begin to perceive themselves, and are perceived by others, as 'failures' at writing before the age that they should actually be formally learning to write.

WHAT CAN WE DO ABOUT IT?

There is nothing we as teachers can do about the age academic schooling begins. It is crucial, therefore, that teachers and other adults working with pupils below the age of seven ensure that the children in their care are learning predominantly through high quality experiences, similar to those found in the areas of learning within the best of Foundation Stage settings, and that everything possible is done to protect and raise self-esteem and self-belief.

Furthermore, we must ensure that the learning that occurred for 4 and 5 year olds in the Foundation Stage and Year 1 phases of English schools is recycled in Year 2 and throughout Key Stage 2.

7.iii   THE IMPORTANCE OF RECYCLING
There is a well used homily in England that buses always come in threes.

Sadly they don't in education! Buses vital to the development of writing skills pass through most Reception, Year 1 and Year 2 classes at high speed, and many never come back! Many little boys and some little girls are not ready to get onto these buses at age 4 and 5, and some are still not ready at 6. They arrive in Key Stage 2, therefore, with serious gaps in their learning.

Crucial skills that frequently remain underdeveloped through many boys (and some girls) meeting formal learning too early include:

- Handwriting, particularly the correct starting point and way to draw each letter in order to develop a fluent and neat cursive style later on. Sadly, once shaping a letter the 'wrong' way becomes embedded it is very hard to correct.

- Holding a writing tool in the best way to facilitate a neat and accurate writing style. A significant number of boys write with tools held like daggers and it is extremely difficult to change this once it is embedded.

- Spelling, particularly the sight words on the word lists for Reception and Key Stage 1 in the National Literacy Strategy (NLS). There are too many words on these lists for some children aged between four and six, however, they are a crucial contributor towards future success. These lists include the basic words that make up over 25% of all reading and writing. All children should know them by sight, and not have to build them phonetically. (For example; I, and, we, on, at, for, he, is, said, go, you, are, this etcetera)

- Phonics, particularly basic phonic skills to tackle unknown words. Thus later learning in phonics, when the child is now ready and able to learn, does not have a secure foundation.

- Essential use of the full stop and capital letter to demarcate a basic sentence.

As the curriculum moves towards creativity (a most welcome and significant change), it is imperative that teachers recycle the Basic Skills from the age when all pupils are ready for formal learning, that is seven. We recommend they are addressed through five ten minute slots, one per day, throughout Key Stage 2. (See Chapter 8, 'The Importance of Basic Skills').

The writer also recommends the inclusion of times tables for mathematics as a basic skill.

 NB These Basic Skill sessions must be fast, lively and fun.

7.iv   THE IMPORTANCE OF STRUCTURE AND CLARITY

Boys like structure and scaffolds. They enjoy showing success at something they understand and feel confident with, (as do girls of course). Much of our teaching of the 'writing voice' and of generic writing skills, is not structured in clear enough small steps for most boys and some girls to access it. Boys do particularly well in subjects that have a clear and progressive structure, such as mathematics and science. If teachers can identify the small steps in a process and teach them sequentially boys will achieve much better. The small steps identified in The Criterion Scale and also in Chapter 5.v 'Child Friendly Small Step Targets for Big Writing' will assist in this process. (See also Chapter 4, 'What Is Effective Target Setting?')

In addition, teachers need to change boys' self belief that they are 'no good' at writing. This needs to be brought out into the open and acknowledged by skillful teachers who will actually tell boys that it is not their fault that they have developed this negative self image in writing. We need to be open and admit that we have failed them as learners, and that we are now going to re address the issues. This appeals to boys' sense of fairness and begins the process of re-education as writers.

We then need to explain clearly and simply the precise next steps that will enable the child to move forward and make immediate progress, and to show them how and where they can achieve success. Given this clear structure, combined with enhanced self-belief and a lack of 'blame', pupils will thrive and show rapid progress.

We need to make every pupil who does not have a significant special need that impacts on writing, for example motor skills, sight or hearing difficulties, unmanaged ADHD or some aspects of the Autism spectrum, believe that he or she is potentially a Level 4/5 writer and that we are going to enable them to get to that level.

These factors are the success of 'Big Writing'! ('Raising Standards in Writing' 2002 and 'Strategies for Immediate Impact on Writing Standards' 2003.) Schools should implement the teaching methodology and philosophy of 'Big Writing' systematically throughout the school, as a proven way of exciting all pupils, and particularly boys, about writing.

THE WRITER BELIEVES THAT CLOSE TO 90% OF MAINSTREAM PUPILS COULD ACHIEVE LEVEL 4 OR ABOVE IF THEY WERE CONSISTENTLY LEARNING THROUGH BIG WRITING IN THEIR PRIMARY SCHOOLS.

7.v   THE JOSHUA CASE STUDY REVISITED

Joshua's progress from a Level 2c to a Level 4c within three teaching months in Year 6 (January to April 30th 2003) is celebrated in our courses. It is worth returning to this case study in order to consider the significant impact of self-belief on boys' achievement.

CASE STUDY 2 : JOSHUA FIELDHOUSE

Usher Street Primary School is an average sized primary school close to the heart of Bradford. It is an old Victorian building set in a small, entirely concrete playground walled in by Yorkshire stone walls with metal fencing on top. The children are drawn from predominantly rented terraced property. Fifty percent are low socio-economic white English heritage and fifty percent are mixed heritage, predominantly of Asian and Afro-Caribbean heritages and also of low socio-economic background. Poverty is an identified major contributor to underachievement in writing.

Joshua grew up in the narrow streets around Usher Street, and his schooling was entirely in this school. Like many boys across the country, he believed he was 'no good' at writing. The first example of writing that follows (Sample 1) was Joshua's writing in January of 2003. He was in Year 6, and was part of a cohort that had a target of 23% of pupils achieving Level 4 or above for writing. In reality, the school felt only 5 of the 30 pupils (17%) in the cohort were on track to achieve the expected Level 4 or above in writing.

The writer was originally bought in as a consultant by the former South Bradford Education Action Zone to raise that level of achievement. She guaranteed to at least double the expected result (she guarantees to increase standards by 20% or more in the year of introduction of 'Big Writing').

The teaching of the six lessons, spread three weeks apart, with the teacher consolidating and widening the range of examples whilst changing the text type for writing each week (see Chapter 1.ii, 'What is Big Writing?') is described in the 2003 publication, 'Strategies for Immediate Impact on Writing' which includes all the lesson plans and resources used for highly successful intervention. Many teachers have used these effectively in schools during the last four years. The method, when implemented in full, has never failed to increase predicted writing scores at Level 4 and above by 20% or more. The lesson plans and resources are all published in 'Strategies for Immediate Impact on Writing Standards', and also are now available on CD to better enable teachers to overwrite them and personalise them for their class.

Consider Joshua's baseline letter below, written in January 2003. If Joshua was in your Year 6 class, aged 10, in January of the academic year he is to take the tests, what would you be saying about him as a writer?

SAMPLE 1: JOSHUA'S BASELINE JANUARY 2003

When assessing Sample 1, the reader should be concerned that the language that we appreciate in Joshua's writing is not his own, but drawn from the stimulus material. His basic skills of handwriting and sentence punctuation are weak, and the piece is too short to make secure judgements on many aspects of writing. The judgement has to be, therefore, that he is writing at Level 2C. This judgement is confirmed through use of the Criterion Scale for assessing writing ('Raising Standards in Writing' 2002 and 'Strategies for Immediate Impact on Writing Standards' 2003, now available on CD Rom).

Most teachers working with a ten year old exhibiting the skill level of Joshua in January 2003, would be saying that he has a special educational need (SEN), and would be seriously considering dis-application from the tests (withdrawal on the basis of SEN). Both Joshua and his school will have decided that he is 'no good' at writing.

Furthermore, by this stage in Year 6 teachers are under great pressure to ensure school targets are met, and many head teachers and local education authority (LEA) personnel, will be saying, 'Stop worrying about your Level 2s now, it is too late for them. Concentrate on getting your Level 3s into Level 4.'

JOSHUA IS A DISAFFECTED PUPIL WHO DOES NOT BELIEVE HE IS 'ANY GOOD' AT WRITING. HE BELIEVES HE CAN'T WRITE AND THE ADULTS AROUND HIM APPEAR TO BELIEVE HE CAN'T WRITE, SO HE CAN'T WRITE!

SAMPLE 2: JOSHUA'S 'SAT' WRITING TEST MAY 2003
Now look at the first page of Joshua's writing test paper, Sample 2. Joshua was awarded a Level 4 for writing in May 2003. He actually wrote one and a half pages. Using the Criterion Scale to assess his writing, it is an early 4C. That means that on different days in response to different stimuli Joshua will fluctuate between a high Level 3 (3a) and a weak Level 4 (4c).

Teacher assessment would more accurately retain Joshua as a Level 3a for a little longer, until he becomes a secure Level 4, however, in a system where a child's attainment is measured on one specific day and a definitive judgement given, Joshua has his entitlement to his Level 4. Prior to 2003 Joshua would not have achieved a Level 4, as accurate, joined handwriting was an essential factor. The re-writing of the assessment systems in 2003 meant that he can now achieve it.

Furthermore the longer task of 2003, the 'story board' acted as a scaffold for Joshua, enabling him to successfully construct his writing, so that when he goes off subject in the last paragraph on this page, he is actually steered back on again. He might not have achieved this if given less support.

Our education system has failed Joshua. If he can make 2 whole levels of progress in the three teaching months leading to the tests, where might he have been had he been taught in a more appropriate way from the age when he was actually ready to become a writer? (See

Suddenly Tim saw a new game advertised in z's game store, he asked his mum 'sandra' if he could have the game, she said yes! He was stood in the queue for like four hours, when the keeper opened up, everyone charged in like a bull in a china shop, They were knocking practically everything in there way down, All the keeper could do was 'Please that cost alot of money'. Everyone got a game 'that game game', there was one left so I and this girl argued over it, I asked where do you live. She said why should I tell you, I demanded an answer Shelt she then said 36 peticuled avenue, which was down the road from me. So I said we'll both put towards it and you can come to my house and play it with me so she did and when she got to my house she said 'mum, dad'....

I was furious, mum said 'I can explain. That's your sister, we put her in a foster home when she was three, that same year you was born, I've wanted to tell you but but well I was scared very scared. I ran to my room and lied down. Eow I thought for a moment and then decided to be friends with her and ask mum and dad to get

Chapter 7.iii 'The Importance of Recycling'). Joshua needed 3 things to succeed:

- He needed changed self-belief with a guarantee that he could succeed

- He needed basic skills; handwriting, spelling and punctuation for basic sentence structure

- He needed VCOP to develop voice and style. (The Four Generic Targets as described in 'Raising Standards in Writing' 2002 and 'Strategies for Immediate Impact on Writing Standards' 2003.)

JOSHUA NOW BELIEVES HE CAN WRITE!

Because Joshua is a very early Level 4, it is most probable that when he entered secondary school he would have regressed to a consistent Level 3. The writer has clear evidence from two years of action based research that over 50 percent of all pupils regress every summer throughout the primary and early secondary phases. Indeed, in most Year 6 classes the regression begins before most pupils leave their primary schools, as the curriculum changes following the May tests and the intense focus on skills is reduced or abandoned.

Until a writer is a secure Level 5, the skills of writing are not always embedded, unless the individual is a secure high level, (upper Level 5/Level 6) reader. Therefore, it is likely that Joshua's English teacher/s in secondary school do not believe that he ever was a Level 4, and that they will have transmitted their expectation of him as a writer to him. It is quite likely, therefore, that Joshua is now once again a disaffected writer in his secondary school.

The elements of Joshua's work in the actual test that earn him the 4c judgement are predominantly his emerging 'voice and style', plus his improved spelling and more mature handwriting. The aspects of his writing that are not yet well enough developed for a Level 4 are the Basic Skills of neat, accurate, joined handwriting, spelling and accurate use of a range of punctuation for basic sentence structure and effect. These skills take a little longer to develop.

Above all, Joshua has been given the belief that he CAN write, through rapid development of the 'writing voice' in 'Big Writing'.

 "IF YOU THINK YOU CAN OR YOU THINK YOU CAN'T YOU ARE PROBABLY RIGHT!"
(Henry Ford)

 NB Usher Street has experienced a change of head teacher and Year 6 teacher since 2003.

**"Friday is Big Writing Day.
The candle flickers all the way.
The music's all around,
Our heads are down,
Working our fingers to the ground.
That's our Big Writing Day!!!"**

Lauren and Adele
Year 6, Crossley Hall Primary School, Bradford.

56 CHAPTER 8:
THE IMPORTANCE OF BASIC SKILLS

 Chapter 8 examines issues around the teaching of Basic Skills and their impact on writing. It also provides a model for recycling Basic Skills and Case Study 3, Paul's writing.

8.i   THE FOUR BASIC SKILLS

There are four Basic Skills that impact on achievement in writing. They are:

- accurate grammatical structures
- handwriting
- spelling – both sight words and phonics
- basic sentence structure shown by use of the full stop followed by a capital letter

These may be given the acronym 'GHASP' (grammar, handwriting, spelling, and punctuation) if they are a serious issue in the school and it is felt that an acronym would be a useful hook for the pupils.

The writer assesses hundreds of pupils' scripts a year. She also scrutinizes hundreds more for accuracy of assessment, and receives feedback from many Senior Managers in schools. She can personally evidence that large numbers of children are being held back as writers through lack of confidence and/or expertise in two or more of the four basic skills.

Almost every day of most adults' lives they read or write the words on the NLS Reception and Key Stage 1 word lists and many days they use facts from the times tables, phonic skills and handwriting. If teachers fail to provide children with these key skills they deprive them of the basic literacy toolkit for adult life.

The work of a Year 6 pupil at Linthwaite Clough JIN School is published below. In Sample 1 (following page) of Paul's work, Basic Skills were below the level of his voice and style because he is focusing so closely on the not previously seen or prepared stimulus and text type. This commonly happens in test situations. This results in the first piece being assessed at Level 4b. When Paul rewrote the piece, correcting his errors and improving his handwriting, the revised piece, Sample 2, achieves Level 5c.

 NB FEW WORDS HAVE BEEN CHANGED IN SAMPLE 2 – THE 'VOICE AND STYLE' ARE EXACTLY AS IN THE FIRST PIECE. ALL CHANGES WERE SELF INITIATED BY PAUL. THE IMPROVEMENT IS THROUGH IMPROVED ACCURACY.

8.ii   BASIC SENTENCE STRUCTURE

If a child is struggling with basic sentence structure (as shown by use of the full stop followed by a capital letter), a skilled writing partner or a TA or teacher should consistently read back every piece of a child's writing with him/her, in order to help him/her to identify the ends of sentences and insert the full stops and capital letters.

There is evidence that many young children do not 'hear' the writing voice clearly inside their heads, and that they will be more successful if they are actively encouraged to speak their writing out loud as they work.

Certainly it makes the identification of sentence endings clearer.

Teachers working with younger children should say, 'I will say what you are going to write for you so that you can hear where the full stops should be. Soon you will be able to say it for yourself.' When the child is confidently speaking what he is writing, he should then be told, 'Soon you will be able to hear that voice inside your head.' The use of the word 'soon' is important as it is a non-judgemental statement that does not make the child feel 'to blame' or guilty.

This should be done alongside the traditional techniques, such as telling the child that full stops are breathing or rest points. The child may be asked to read his/her work only pausing at full stops. Many children will quickly detect where they need to insert full stops to give a pause.

The same technique may be used to establish finger spaces between words for very young children. The adult says, 'We will say your writing out loud and I will tap the table each time you need to put your finger down and move along. When this is established, the teacher says, 'Soon you will be able to say it out loud without my help.' Then, 'Soon you will be able to hear it inside your head'. In this way, the child moves forward in very small, achievable steps. (See Chapter 5, 'The Process of Target Setting in Big writing').

8.iii   SMALL-STEP TARGETS

The two following examples exemplify use of small-step targets. Teachers would normally identify the whole target as one step:

✛ **Target 1:** Use full stops and capital letters to show sentences.

✛ **Target 2:** Use finger spaces between words.

These types of targets can usually be broken down into smaller steps. The smaller the step the more likely the child is to achieve it. The examples above might now look like this:

✛ **Target 1**

Step 1: Can you tap the table when you hear the end of a sentence when I read your work out loud?

Step 2: Can you put in a full stop when you hear the end of a sentence when I read your work out loud?

Step 3: Can you always put a capital letter after every full stop? (May be subsumed into Step 2 if the child is able to cope, so that both full stop and capital letter are addressed at the same time.)

SAMPLE 1: PAUL'S UNEDITED WRITING.

Sample 1

3-2-05

Paul 4b

ALIEN!

I was bored, I often was. I sauntered up the pavement loitering outside shops. Living in a village isolated from the rest of the world, well thats how I saw it anyway It was hard. No one else was around, then I heard foot steps around the corner came a man, he had skinny long legs, he wore a skirt and had an orange gear on his left cheek. He didn't look like a man, but I knew he was when I heard his voice:"He-110" he said. It was a deep, creaky voice, "I'm... Amy" AMY! "I'm a man," MAN, men aren't called Amy. "You must be a I'm a boy.
woman" WHATA "Do You want to be my friend?
N.P ✓
I didn't know what to say. "Yeah, Sure" I replied
After that I walked off.

Later, I turned round. ~~He~~. He was follow me.

"Thats my house," He pointed over on to the horizon. There was a weird shape, I went to investigate. By the time we arrived it was dark, or getting dark.
"This?" I said
"Yes, I'm an A-L-I-E-N"

✓ I enjoyed this!

Sample 2   Paul (5c)

ALIEN!

I was bored, I offten was. I sauntered
up the pavement, loitering outside shops.
Living in a village isolated from the
rest of the world was hard. Well
that's how I saw it anyway. NO
one else was around, but then I
heard footsteps.

Seconds later I looked round,
around the corner came a man
with skinny legs and a skirt, with
an orange scar on his cheek.
He didn't look like a man, but
I knew he was when he spoke.
"He-110", he said in a deep
croaky voice. "I'm... Amy." 'Amy'
I thought. "I'm a man," 'Man'
I thought. 'Men aren't called Amy'
"You must be a woman," he said to
me. 'What?' I thought.
"I'm a boy" I shouted.
"NO difference really, do you
want to be my friend?" He asked.
I didn't know what to say.

Step 4: Can you put in the full stops and capital letters when saying your own writing out loud?

Step 5: Can you put in capital letters and full stops when you are 'saying' your writing inside your head?

✛ **Target 2:** Please tell me what you want to write

Step 1: Can you put down your finger and move along for the next word when I say what you want to write and I tap the table after each word?

Step 2: Can you put down your finger and move along for the next word when you are saying aloud what you want to write?

Step 3: Can you put down your finger and move along for the next word when you are 'saying' your writing inside your head?

Scaffolding the child's learning into clear small steps in this way makes it easier for the child to be successful. The child should not move on to the next step until they are confident at the previous one.

The adult who knows the child's ability best should be the one who decides how small the steps need to be for the child. (See also Chapter 5 'The Process of Target Setting in Big Writing').

8.iv HANDWRITING
Schools should expect all children to develop neat, joined writing by the time they leave Key Stage 1. If we expect one hundred percent we will get much closer to it than if we say not all pupils can get there.

The particular style taught in a school is not the most important aspect, as long as it achieves a neat, flowing and legible hand. The most important factor is the consistency with which all adults teach and promote the school style, using it in every aspect of their work in school.

Boys have a great sense of fairness. Girls also have a huge sense of fairness, but they will often persevere even when they consider something to be unfair. Many boys and some girls may be disaffected by a perceived lack of fairness. Teachers saying that all pupils must do something one way (for example handwriting), and then doing it a different way themselves (and not always neatly), can be regarded as unfair by boys. It is crucial, therefore, that every adult consistently models the school's style as they write within the classroom for any purpose.

Every child should be taught handwriting pro-actively for as long as is necessary for her/him to develop a neat and flowing, joined style. They should then be given interesting activities to consolidate their style (see

Chapter 8.x, 'Recycling Basic Skills'). At the beginning of every new term (or half term if the priority is high) all pupils should be taken back to basic letter formation and first joining patterns, addressing the full process within two weeks to arrive back to the point at which they are currently working.

A talented Teaching Assistant (TA) who is a good modeller of the school style, could also run a six week intervention clinic at the beginning of each year for high priority pupils in Key Stage 2. These might be daily for 10 minutes or twice weekly for twenty minutes. (See also Chapter 8.x and Appendix 4, the 'Write on Track' Intervention.)

8.v SPELLING
The NLS word lists for the years previous to the year a child is in should be recycled intensively at the beginning of each year, or re-taught through one ten minute session a week. How many teachers actually know which of the words in the preceding word lists all the children in their class actually know? This is a basic entitlement similar to times tables in mathematics, and we are depriving many children of this entitlement.

THIS LEARNING MUST BE LIVELY AND FUN.

Making recycled learning turgid is akin to punishing learners for something that is not their fault. It is our education system that has caused their difficulties, and we must accept responsibility for it. Furthermore, disaffected pupils will not be re-motivated by rote learning and repetitive exercises. We should devise interesting and enjoyable ways for pupils to access the learning they have missed.

In addition the current word list, Year 5 if the pupil is in Year 5, should also be taught in a separate session, and a further session should address phonics. As with handwriting, every term or half term the teaching of phonics should revert to the very beginning, with a two week review of basic letter sounds, blends, diagraphs and initial and final sounds. (See Chapter 8.x 'Recycling the Basic Skills').

8.vi GRAMMATICAL STRUCTURES
Accuracy of grammar is better addressed through oral activities (the development of the 'posh voice') and through the imaginary friend (see below).

'Talking Posh' is a fun and effective way to address grammatical errors.

IF A CHILD CAN'T SAY IT A CHILD CAN'T WRITE IT!

Children who have a strong local accent will have distorted spelling when they do not know a word by sight, and they try for it phonetically. This is because they are writing in their 'speaking voice'. Look at Liam's writing below. The last line is written entirely with a Yorkshire accent: 'Ol you did wos sot tere' = 'All you did was sat there'.

approach to building a 'writing voice' and enjoy the VCOP oral activities through 'talking posh'. This develops the model for higher order language structures to be used in writing.

Children who talk with a local dialect, who are bilingual and are therefore bringing structures from first language to their English, or children who speak in patois, show grammatical errors in writing because they are hearing their 'speaking' voice inside their head. Clearly, if children already speak with 100% accuracy this is not an issue, but they may still enjoy the fun

Tell pupils they need to write with a 'posh' voice that is different from their writing voice. Stress that we like the way they talk and are not trying to change that (this is important for self-esteem and sometimes even for 'survival' within their community) Nevertheless, inside our heads we need a 'posh' voice for writing.

8.vii WHAT IS TALKING POSH?

'Talking posh' is actually another accent; however, it enables a fun focus on grammatical structures and pronunciation.

The writer usually introduces 'posh talk' through role play, using fun scenarios in an 'Upstairs Downstairs' type of setting. She quickly moves it into introducing one 'posh' lesson a week, where she teaches through 'posh talk', pupils respond to questions in 'posh talk' and a discussion activity is built into the lesson, which must be conducted in 'posh talk'. In all these scenarios, all pupils who are not speaking at any given moment are 'the speech police' and shout a correction if they spot a grammatical or pronunciation error. Naturally the teacher makes the most errors, and pupils greatly enjoy the fun of correcting her/him.

This lively lesson is moved through different subjects week by week, to keep it 'fresh' and enjoyable. It is complimented by stocking fillers using higher order VCOP skills in a posh voice, for example the Level 5 structure at the opening of the book and the following:

Example 1: "Despite wishing to succeed as a writer, I continue to struggle with my illegible handwriting."
(Open with connectives and use 'wow' words)

Example 2: "Anxiously I awaited the return of my writing to ascertain whether it had improved."
(Open with 'ly' words and use 'wow' words)

Example 3: "Succeeding as a writer has become of paramount importance to me."
(Open with 'ing' words and use 'wow' words)

Example 4: "Anxiously awaiting the return of the test papers..."
(Open with an 'ly' word and follow with an 'ing' word)

Example 5: "Having anxiously awaited..."
(Open with an 'ing' word and follow with an 'ly' word)

'Posh talk' can also be reinforced through the teacher's 'imaginary friend'.

8.viii   WHAT IS THE IMAGINARY FRIEND?

An imaginary friend is a huge asset in the classroom! He is not just a source of fun... he is an invaluable teaching tool!

The imaginary friend 'sits' on an empty chair at the front of the classroom and the teacher talks to him as though he was real, and 'listens' to his answers before relating them to the class. The imaginary friend (who has a name that it is unlikely will ever belong to a real pupil in the school, e.g. Marmaduke or Archibald) serves the following crucial purposes:

1. He answers all the questions that no-one in the class can answer, and also the questions where the teacher wants a quick answer as he/she only posed the question to set the children thinking. This positive behaviour endears the imaginary friend to the class and gives him an acceptable identity.

2. He makes all the mistakes that pupils in the class make, so protecting their self-esteem. When the teacher identifies an issue in the work of one or more pupils, such as lack of punctuation, low level writing, overuse of a skill, inaccurate grammar or misuse of vocabulary, the teacher produces a fake piece from the imaginary friend that replicates the mistake. Pupils are then asked to help the friend to understand what he has done wrong or overused, and so learn themselves in a none threatening and entertaining way. The errors are produced in a written context, either on OHT, interactive whiteboard or in paper form (in which case pupils might discuss the errors and feed back orally, or use highlighters to identify errors, or insert using a pencil).

3. He makes grammatical errors in speech or writing, which the teacher repeats to the class and asks them to discuss them and agree what the correct structure would have been.

4. He writes at low levels and the class discuss how he could move his writing up one or more level, (up-levelling). He then writes at the higher level to demonstrate to the pupils how good their advice was. This strategy is also an excellent vehicle for explicitly teaching what each level looks like and what its characteristics are. Children should be able to 'guesstimate' levels of writing and explain their judgements, in order to bring this knowledge to assessment of their own writing.

Discussion around the grammatical errors made by the imaginary friend, plus pupils' peer assessment of his work, provide a lively and effective way of tackling the common grammatical errors made by the rest of the class.

The teacher may then refer back to the imaginary friend's mistakes prior to the next writing session, saying;

"And be careful not to make Marmaduke's mistakes! Do you remember when he...?"

Because the imaginary friend is a boy, he alternates between being a positive role model for the boys and making 'boy typical' errors. This strategy is none threatening for the boys, a real source of humour for the class and highly effective in impact.

EXAMPLE OF EXCELLENT INCLUSION OF THE IMAGINARY FRIEND

Crossley Hall Primary School is situated in Bradford. The Year 6 teachers adopted the strategies of Big Writing, with excellent impact. This included seating for an imaginary friend in 6N, whom Mrs. Naylor (class teacher) named ARNOLD.

It takes courage to maintain a sense of fun throughout an OFSTED inspection, but in the Spring Term of 2004, when Crossley Hall was inspected, the empty seat remained at the front of the classroom for Arnold's use in Big Writing (and other lessons too!).

Part way through the inspection an inspector bustled into the classroom, and seeing the empty chair assumed it was for him. As he began to sit down there was a loud gasp and as one the class shouted,

"You've sat on ARNOLD!"

That lesson was given the grade 1 for excellence by the inspector.

The pupils of Crossley Hall wrote some excellent letters to the writer. An excerpt from one is published here.

Perhaps he is 'having a laugh' at the writer's expense!

EXCERPT OF A LETTER FROM A PUPIL OF CROSSLEY HALL

Dear Mrs Wilson

What a pleasure it has been to be apart of your project.

I can just remember when we were writing Level 2 to 3 and then, on the 12th December you came with V.C.O.P to save the day. (and personally you have been my Saviour for Literacy this year.)

One of the most important things you have taught me this year, has got to be believing in myself. At the beginning of the year, I thought I was going to get a level 5. The other thing you have given me is the tools for me to do well in Literacy for as long as I live.

I honestly believe that you have made us a team not a set. Mind you We are the brainest set in school despite the fact what Mrs Naylor and his set think. You taught me to be proud of my work Which I am but also you have made me improving my attitude to work.

But now everything I write dosn't come from the brain it comes from the heart

8.x   RECYCLING BASIC SKILLS

Year 3 is a very important year in terms of re-affecting the disaffected, as all children are now at the age where they are ready to learn. Teaching in Year 3 must be lively and challenging, but should re-address the key skills associated with all subjects at the opening of each Unit of Study. Key Stage 2 teachers (and especially Year 3 teachers) need a clear picture of how children learn in the early years, and all the skills they should develop as a foundation for further learning. Too many teachers in Key Stage 2 dismiss the teaching of basic skills as being the 'job' of the Foundation Stage and Key Stage 1, and do not understand the importance of offering children a fresh chance to learn these skills. This leads to many boys and some girls being trapped at a low skill level, and reinforces the self-belief that they are 'no good' at something.

TOO MANY CHILDREN, PARTICULARLY BOYS, ARE TRAPPED WITHIN LEVEL 2 BY WEAK BASIC SKILLS, LACK OF LENGTH AND DETAIL IN THEIR WRITING AND THE BELIEF THAT THEY ARE 'NO GOOD' AT WRITING.
(See Case Study 1; 'Joshua Fieldhouse' in Chapter 7, 'The Difference Between Boys and Girls').

Teachers wrongly make assumptions that pupils get bored by recycling because we, as adults, do. It is sedentary and unimaginative teaching that bores children. All skills can and should be recycled through new contexts. It is the using and applying in a range of contexts that embeds skills and confirms learning.

The table below suggests an effective formula for addressing these crucial life skills. In addition, however, the basic skill of accurate grammatical structures must be addressed through talk, as previously explained (see 8.vi 'Grammatical Structures').

We recommend 5 ten-minute Basic Skills Sessions, one each day, throughout Key Stage 2. These should be lively and fun, and should recycle basic skills continuously across the four years, returning briefly at the beginning of each term to the very first steps in each skill and moving briskly forward to each pupil's current point of performance.

RECYCLING BASIC SKILLS

The 10 minute a day sessions for all children in Key Stage 2.
The numbering does not dictate the sequence, it is an organisational device only.

⏱ DAY	✎ BASIC SKILL
1	Spelling - sight words: Recycle word lists from Reception to the year preceding the year pupils are now in. Thus if pupils are in Year 5, list Reception to Year 4. This should be done in lively, fun ways. The following are examples of how this might be done. Make into laminated playing cards and use to play games such as 'snap' or the matching game using 2 identical sets. Cards should be put into differentiated sets with some words from all years involved in every set. Children say the words together as they are turned over.
2	Spelling - phonics: Recycle skills in phonics from Reception to a level of confident selection strategies. The whole school must conform to the same method and approaches. The method chosen is not as important as the uniformity. By the time pupils are confident in all phonics they should be using and applying them. The following are two ways this might be done: In 2s/3s pupils make up complex 'nonsense' words, and identify humorous meanings to them. The class group select the one they find most amusing and then each child spells the word (Personal whiteboards and markers?) as s/he thinks it might be. They then explain their strategies and source words, and the teacher contributes any possibilities not previously considered. They then agree the most likely and record. Alternatively, pupils use dictionaries to locate and record complex words they think will be unknown to their peers. The teacher then says each word in turn (avoids mispronunciation difficulties) and pupils attempt to spell it, explaining their strategies. They then try to guess the meaning.

⏱ DAY	✏ BASIC SKILL
2 cont	At the beginning of each term, pupils in Key Stage 2 should be taken back rapidly through the early parts of the phonics journey, sounding single letters, blends, diagraphs etcetera over a two session period at most. This provides a recycling opportunity for those who need it.
3	Spelling: sight words. The sight words for the current year, as dictated by the national strategies. These might be taught in more traditional ways through flash cards, 'look, cover, say', air writing to the upper left, (brain based learning) and spelling games and activities. For an effective adaptation of air writing see Appendix 4 'Write on Track'.
Handwriting: The style chosen is not the most important factor, it is that every adult in the school consistently models it in all their writing, and teaches it consistently using the same language and methods.

When pupils have an established neat, accurate and joined style, it is practised through presentation skills in interesting contexts, e.g. recording a piece of their own work that they are proud of, building an anthology of poems they enjoy, making a personal study on a self-selected research topic or producing a greeting card for a special occasion.

At the beginning of each term, pupils in Key Stage 2 should be taken back rapidly through the early parts of the handwriting journey, forming single letters, blends and diagraphs before moving briskly to the point they are now at, over a period of not more than two handwriting sessions. This provides a recycling opportunity for those who need it. |
| 5 | NUMERACY! TIMES TABLES! Every pupil is expected to know every times table by the end of Year 5 (National Numeracy Strategy). Teach times tables proactively and give pupils exciting ways to develop this and other key basic skills. (See 'THE MATHSDOCTOR' page on our website, www.twentytwentyvision.org.uk NB In the revised NHS all must be known by end of Year 4. |

8.xi   THE IMPORTANCE OF WHOLE STAFF INSET FOR BASIC SKILLS

It is crucial that at the opening of each academic year time is allocated to re-address the agreed whole-school methods for teaching Basic Skills, and that all staff not only model during their teaching but also use in all their work with pupils. All staff, both teaching and support, should use the school's style of handwriting, spell and punctuate accurately and speak in standard English. We are the role models for children and we need to be consistent.

Head teachers should expect that staff will need to be inducted into the school way of doing things, and should provide opportunity for colleagues to retrace the learning journey from its very beginning once a year, and to practise the skill themselves. If asked whether anyone is still unsure how to teach a basic skill, some staff may find it difficult to identify personal need publicly. All staff, therefore, need to go through the process, which should only take the equivalent of a staff meeting or one session on an INSET day.

8.xii   'WRITE ON TRACK':

'Write on Track' is an intervention planned to raise standards for pupils trapped at Level 2 in Lower Key Stage 2. It is intended to be implemented for between six and eight weeks although a very small number of pupils may stay on it longer. Normally it should replace the literacy hour for that period.

This intervention is based upon intensive re-teaching of basic skills and up-levelling through VCOP. It should always be made lively and fun.

The intervention itself is provided as Appendix 4 at the back of this publication.

**"Today is Big Writing Day,
Year 6 are shouting hooray!
The lights go dim,
And work begins,
I wouldn't want to be away!"**

Ryan and Thomas
Year 6, Crossley Hall Primary School, Bradford.

66 CHAPTER 9:
WHAT REALLY DOES RAISE STANDARDS IN WRITING?

 Chapter 9 examines issues around how children develop a higher order writing voice and why many teachers continue to believe that the solution is to improve reading. It also provides a model for raising standards in eight weeks in a Year 6 class.

9.i   HOW DO WE DEVELOP THE 'WRITING VOICE'?
Most teachers believe that to improve writing we need to improve reading.

If you ask teachers who taught them the Level 5+ skills that they use in writing, most cannot name a teacher who did this. They usually remember being taught to take writing to pieces, but not how to structure it with a higher order 'voice'.

An example of the higher order writing voice:

'Having ascertained that the majority of the pupils were insecure in their basic skills, the teacher determined that intervention was essential.'

Most teachers, on reflection, will say they acquired the more sophisticated structures of Level 5+ from reading rather than from explicit teaching. This leads them to believe that in order to improve writing we must first improve reading. One might assume, therefore, that most people who go on to higher education not only read widely at a high level, but also have a subconscious that enjoys language and stores a vast repertoire of words, phrases and structures for later use.

The evidence is, however, that 50% or more of pupils will never read widely enough, with enough enjoyment or at a high enough level to impact on their writing. The eleven-plus test was designed to cream off the pupils who have the potential to become professional and provide them with an academic education, whilst pupils who were not deemed capable of achieving graduate status were given a more appropriate education for working life. If we use the eleven plus as an indicator of potential for academic achievement and a career in one of the 'professions', then between 25% and 40% of the population were deemed to have that potential.

Grammar schools and independent schools have traditionally set great store by reading, exposing their pupils to a wide range of classical and contemporary literature. Furthermore, many students have grown up with a love of reading, often because of the influence of the home environment. The writer maintains that their pupils developed the 'writing voice' through this exposure and not through explicit teaching of grammar and text types, and completion of grammar exercises.

Younger children develop the voice when they grow up in homes where literature is valued and where they read and are read to. They develop understanding of language structures mainly through listening to and participating in extended dialogue. The amount of literature read in depth in primary schools has reduced significantly over the past ten years, due to pressures of the national curriculum and to literacy being taught within tight time frames with an average of twenty minutes on a given aspect. The National Literacy Strategy model frequently promotes working from short excerpts of text. The rebirth of creativity in the curriculum is also seeing a welcome return of the daily 'story' slot towards the end of the day.

To glean structures for a high Level 4 or Level 5, a pupil would need to be reading at length from texts written at Level 5 or above. Most primary school age children have not had that opportunity in recent years, and even if they did have the opportunity, a significant proportion would be unable to access writing at those levels.

In addition, the pupil would need to have the type of subconscious that is excited by language, has good understanding of how it works (although they need not know the technical terminology) and stores higher order structures for later use. This is clearly how the subconscious of the majority of those who achieve academically works, but a significant percentage of the population do not evidence this behaviour.

The skills of writing are currently taught predominantly through showing pupils examples of text and expecting them to absorb, retain, and later use and apply the skills demonstrated. Teaching skills in the literacy hour through access to technical terminology, and then practising use of the skills in de-contextualised activities, does not embed them nor does it give pupils sufficient ownership to use and apply them in a range of different contexts throughout their lives. This process is about analysis of writing rather than about composition.

9.ii   THE IMPORTANCE OF OWNERSHIP
Ownership is a crucial element of a pupil's confidence in deploying skills in writing.

Almost every child in the land can quote significant phrases from a range of traditional tales and verse, for example:

'Trip trap, trip trap, who's that crossing over my bridge?'

'Fee, fie, fo, fum. I smell the blood of an English man.'

'I'll huff and I'll puff and I'll blow your house down.'

Young children do not, however, 'own' those phrases, they perceive them to be the words of the character who spoke them. Consequently they do not usually use all or any part of the phrase in their own work. In actual fact, 'trip trap' and 'huff and puff' would be delightful phrases to find in a seven year old's writing. Almost every seven year old in England knows them, but would not think to transfer them into his/her personal writing unless they are retelling the original story they met them in.

9iii   WHAT CAN WE DO?

We need to teach children explicitly that it is not only alright, it is actually 'good' to 'steal' from other people's writing and use the structures in our own writing. After all, this is what WE teachers did and are continuing to do throughout our adult life!

Every time we put up a piece of text for any purpose in any subject, we should ask pupils to skim it first and see if there is any exciting use of VCOP ('Raising Standards in Writing' 2002 and 'Strategies for Immediate Impact on Writing' 2003). New vocabulary should be 'discovered' and owned by the children themselves through 'stealing'. They should immediately be asked to own it by making up oral sentences using the new word or phrase. The word should then be recorded on card, including the name of the child who first 'stole' it, and displayed in the VCOP display on the wall around the main teaching white or black board.

Thus we are teaching children to do consciously what we as teachers have been doing sub-consciously throughout our lives.

Throughout the week, every week, all words and phrases should be 'played with' through oral composition in any spare minutes at beginnings and ends of lessons, for example while lining up for PE, waiting for the hall to be free, waiting for the bell for break etcetera. (See Chapter 1.xi, 'What Are Stocking Fillers?')

Trawling text to find good examples of VCOP for children to 'find' can be highly time consuming. The writer finds it not only quicker but more effective to write her own text for pupils' use in Big Writing sessions. Thus she can ensure that they will 'find' what she wants them to find! Pupils enjoy using highlighters to identify words and phrases they would be interested in stealing, and then narrowing the choice to one example each, which they have to justify by explaining their choice. Examples of this are included in 'Strategies for Immediate Impact on Writing Standards'.

Teaching pupils the writing voice orally, through 'Big Writing', has been proved to enable all pupils who do not have a significant special need to compose higher order language structures. They are then told, "If you use that when you write you will score big goals and go up the league table."

Analyse the higher order structure used at the opening of this chapter:

'Having ascertained that the majority of the pupils were insecure in their basic skills, the teacher determined that intervention was essential.'

In 'Big Writing' terms this is explained as:

a. Open with an 'ing' word.
b. Use ambitious vocabulary.

9.iv   THREE IMMEDIATE IMPACT STRATEGIES

There are three ways to have an immediate impact on standards in Year 6 classes:

1. Use the six lesson plans and resources from 'Strategies for Immediate Impact on Writing Standards' in the period from January to May of the test year.

2. Use the model provided below for impact in 8 weeks.

3. If you do nothing else, concentrate daily on use of connectives and openers, particularly opening with connectives, 'ly' words and 'ing' words, and the Punctuation Pyramid and its associated games. In addition, flood the children's lives with ambitious vocabulary for however little time you have prior to the tests. (Impact in two or more weeks).

See Chapter 8. vii 'What is Talking Posh?' for examples.

⏱ QUICK IMPACT IN 8 WEEKS

This model is designed for Year 6 teachers who meet Big Writing in March of the test year. It is still possible to raise standards within this time scale through the following intervention:
You will need:

1. Loads of energy (essential).
2. Support to make resources (desirable).
3. Money to buy special portfolios and pens (desirable).
4. A Mozart track and a CD/cassette player (essential).
5. A very large candle in a tin holder with rocks round for stability (essential).
6. A way to dim the classroom lighting (essential).
7. Edible 'goals' as rewards (essential).
8. Enthusiasm, commitment, belief and perseverance (essential).

⏱	📋 **Quick Impact in eight weeks for Year 6**
Once a week for 5 weeks	Weekly 'Big Writing' lesson. Duration 1 and half hours split exactly in half by playtime (morning) **Session 1:** series of fast, fun, oracy based activities around VCOP for 35 minutes plus 10 minutes to jot thoughts down – choice of ways **Session 2:** 'Big Writing' – pupils write in silence. Softened lighting, candle and Mozart. Portfolios and pens on desks, plus A4 lined paper with margin Change the text type every week (see Chapter 1.vii, 'Changing the Text Type'). Use time prompts to ensure use of VCOP (see Day 5, Appendix 4 'Write on Track'). Use the chant before each piece of writing, (see Chapter 1.vi, 'The Chant as a Hook').
Afternoon before 'Big Writing'	As late as possible (before or after 'story'): introduce stimulus for next day, and the text type to be used. Show and remind of characteristics of text type and discuss stimulus. (15 minutes)
Days leading up to 'Big Writing'	Frequent, fast fun activities on VCOP, ('stocking fillers') lasting between a few minutes (Who can make me up….) to 10 / 15 minutes (up-levelling activities / helping Damian etc). (See Chapter 1.xi 'What Are Stocking Fillers?'
Day after 'Big Writing'	Celebration of successes / Goal Scorers 10 to 15 minutes at any time of day. (See 'Strategies for Immediate Impact on Writing Standards').Pupils highlight own VCOP. Compare 2 pieces of writing for 'Let's play spot the difference', etc. Compare the 3 pieces produced that week. Are all 3 at same high level for both 'whats' and both 'Hows'. **1:** What = text type **2:** What = stimulus **3:** How = basic skills **4:** How = writing voice
Additional writing session	For another subject, using another text type probably history, geography, science or design and technology. Use the chant as a hook. Pre- prepare in a previous session for that subject. End of afternoon before review stimulus and text type as for main session. Dim lighting, candle and Mozart. Pupils write for 45 minutes. Counts as that subject's time. e.g. Persuasive letter on environmental issue for geography Instructional or explanation text for science or D&T Report for history or geography etc. One further text type per week for another subject as above under 'Big Writing' conditions One 'short piece' per week in another subject session, changing text type, under 'BW' conditions Stocking Fillers and Up-levelling throughout the week.
Once a week for final weeks (3)	Change structure to 35 minutes before play and 50/55 minutes after play. Session 1: 35 minutes, fast, fun, oracy based as previously. Session 2: Sample test conditions to write previously 'unseen' long piece. Retain dim lighting, Mozart and candle.

📌 **NB** BEFORE EVERY 'BW' SESSION YOU MUST ASK CLASS TO DO THE 'WHAT HAVE WE GOT TO REMEMBER – THE VCOP' CHANT.

"Big Writing is the thing for me,
It fills me with oh so much glee!
I write 'til I drop,
I don't want to stop,
'Cos V.C.O.P. is the key!"

Isabella and Claire,
Year 5, Crossley Hall Primary School, Bradford.

70 **CHAPTER 10:**
CASE STUDIES

Case Study 1 is 'The British Army School, Bishopspark' in Chapter 3.

Case Study 2 is the 'Return to Joshua' Case Study in Chapter 4, 'The Difference Between Boys and Girls'.

Case Study 3 is Paul's work in chapter 8, 'The importance of basic skills'.

The following are a further nine further case studies from schools who have been generous enough to share their outstanding successes with the writer.

CASE STUDY 4
HEATON PRIMARY SCHOOL, BRADFORD

Heaton Primary School is a large 3 form entry school on the outskirts of Bradford. Raising attainment in writing has featured on the School Improvement Plan for three years.

Zoe Mawson is the Assistant Head teacher. She sent us the following commentary:

"Three years ago we were struggling to motivate children into achieving high quality written work, particularly boys. Attainment was well below that of reading, and the rate of progress was also slower, so the gap was widening.

We first became involved with the Ros. Wilson strategy, when we had a drive to improve assessment techniques and so we decided to use the Criterion Scale to mark our termly writing assessments. This increased teachers' understanding of the levels as well as the knowledge of the essential features of writing.

At this point, we saw the Ros. Wilson course – promising to have an immediate impact on standards - and made a decision that the Literacy Co-ordinator and a Standard Scale Teacher would attend, with a view to extending the strategy across the school if we felt that it would make a difference. The feedback from the training was extremely positive and Ros. Wilson was very inspirational. The staff were very excited and keen to get going. We shared the strategy with all staff through a series of twilight meetings and made a decision about the implementation, including buying all the candles, music and chocolate. Even though a sweet treat is a little controversial, it has been well worth it and in many classrooms it is not now necessary as the children are self motivated!

Each year group decided to have a Big Writing Day on the same day in order to help the management of the sessions and to build the excitement. Exciting it was! However, we soon realised that we had to change the name from Big Writing to Best Writing as our younger children thought that they had to write very large letters!!

As you walked around school, signs on the classroom doors let everyone know that their class was not to be disturbed (so that the atmosphere was not spoilt!) When you peeped in, the candle glowed, the music was calming and the children were engrossed in their work. All classrooms contained prompts to remind children of the VCOP principle of the strategy. Children really looked forward to Best Writing Day and were annoyed if it had to be missed for any reason. Pupils love the atmosphere in the sessions, but also realise that the strategy helps to improve their writing. Commenting on the strategy, one child said, "When my teacher stops us during the writing, she asks everyone for their best connectives or WOW words and then you can use them in your own writing. That's great!"

We did see an immediate impact in both achievement and in pupils' attitudes to writing. I will never forget one playtime when a Year Six boy – who would have usually used his playtimes rather differently! – ran up to me and said, "You'll never guess what? I used all the level 4 punctuation in my Best Writing today!" He had used the punctuation pyramid as a checklist and was genuinely proud of his efforts, an emotion we had rarely seen.

The table below shows a comparison on progress points made in Writing for the Autumn Term 2003 and the Spring Term 2004 (where the writing strategy had been in place for 1 term). Progress in the Spring Term is above that of National Expectations.

	AUTUMN TERM	SPRING TERM
Year 3 – overall points progress in Writing	0.5	1.9
Year 5 - overall points progress in Writing	1.1	2.4
Year 6 - overall points progress in Writing	1.9	3.1

This rate of progress has continued and our most recent data analysis is showing that, for the first time, attainment in writing is higher than reading in many Year Groups.

We were inspected at the start of the Summer Term 2004 and the strategy was favourably commented upon many times throughout the Ofsted report. It appeared as a strength in Pupils' Attitudes, Values and Other Personal Qualities and the Quality of Education section quoted that:

"This kind of approach has captured the imagination of all pupils, particularly boys, many of whom had previously shown little interest in writing lengthy pieces."

The Head Teacher of the school, Beverley Ledra, is delighted with the strategy:

"I must admit that I questioned the promise made by Ros; that the impact would be immediate, but the results have been extraordinary. Both the children and staff love writing in this way and the introduction of the strategy has resulted in better quality writing throughout the school."

I would recommend this writing strategy to anyone, regardless of the standards of writing in your school. It focuses children on the key skills, providing them with a successful formula, and (almost more importantly) instils a love of writing into all children. It has certainly worked in our school."

Zoe Mawson
Assistant Headteacher
Heaton Primary School
15.3.05

The following are excerpts from Heaton Primary School's OFSTED report for 2004:

- The rigorously organised system adopted by the school for teaching writing, which they call 'Best Writing', has had a massive benefit in terms of achievement particularly for boys, who were previously reluctant to write much at all.

- ...there are many pupils learning English as an additional language who have benefited from the Best Writing project.

- Moments of spirituality occur across the multi-faith assemblies... they also happen in lessons: for example in Best Writing an atmosphere is created with music and candles in which pupils can work silently and do their best.

- The reason why the pupils' achievements in English are very good ... is because the school has adopted a well-known method of teaching writing, which they call Best Writing. The children love it and often sigh when they have to stop. The amount and quality of their work are better than anything they have produced before. In one excellent lesson in Year 6, pupils wrote with such enthusiasm and speed that one pupil had written 60 words almost as soon as the lesson began. This kind of approach has captured the imagination of all pupils...

- Boys have made good progress in writing since the introduction of Best Writing.

- Achievement in writing is very good and, in a few lessons, outstanding. The drive to improve writing standards, particularly those of boys, has developed very successful strategies across the school. Teachers and pupils work very closely together to explore and enrich skills in weekly Best Writing work. After thorough preparation, final writing sessions encourage reflection and care. Quiet music, candles and dimmed lighting give these sessions a special calm and encourage creativity. Pupils experience writing as a craft, and enjoy it because they have many new skills at their fingertips. Pupils, classmates and teachers share in assessment, improving accuracy but also highlighting and praising what is working well. As a result, Year 4 pupils have reached the level expected for their ages. Moreover, the school has all but closed the usual gaps between attainment in reading and writing, and between boys' and girls' achievement in writing.

CASE STUDY 5
MASTER OF TEACHING DEGREE

GAINSBOROUGH PRIMARY SCHOOL, LONDON BOROUGH OF NEWHAM

Gainsborough Primary School is situated in the London Borough of Newham, in an area of high deprivation with approximately 70% of pupils receiving free school meals. The school received a full day's INSET (In-service training) on October 24th 2003 as a result of their identifying the raising of standards in writing as their 'final hurdle' in progressing from Special Measures, through Serious Weaknesses to becoming an LEA (Local Education Authority) 'minimum touch' school. Despite their hard work, standards in writing remained stubbornly 50 % behind those for reading, and thus they took on board the 'Big Writing' programme as a major initiative.

⏱ Timescales:
From January 2003 to March 2004 Janine conducted research with her own class, comparing results with those of the parallel class not undertaking Big writing.

In October 2003 Big Writing was adopted by the whole school following whole-school INSET.

Janine Ryan is a Year 6 teacher at the above school. In the Autumn of 2004 she was awarded her M.Teach. degree, having focused her research on raising standards in writing through Big Writing. The following are excerpts from her final paper.

PRACTICE-BASED ENQUIRY

'The research reported here focused on raising standards in writing in a Year 6 classroom in the London Borough of Newham. The impetus behind the study came from my involvement in a Masters program at the Institute of Education, plus my combined roles in school of Year 6 teacher, Literacy and Assessment Co-ordinators. Our school's OFSTED report in 2001 highlighted past poor performance in writing as a 'Key Issue' resulting in a school wide focus on raising standards in this area. A chance reading of Ros. Wilson's book, 'Raising Standards in Writing' led to adoption of her teaching model within my classroom on a short-term trial basis. The immediate impact of its introduction was tangible and led to the current study to ascertain whether a knowledge of Wilson's four identified strands, namely vocabulary, connectives, sentence openers and punctuation, would raise standards as assessed by Year 6 SATs.

The study began in January 2003 and was completed in March 2004.' (Abstract)

'Currently I am a Year 6 teacher in the London Borough of Newham, with the additional roles of Literacy and

Assessment Co-Ordinators. I am also on the Senior Management Team. As a school we are located within an area of high socio-economic deprivation, with approximately 70% of our children receiving free school meals. Over the past four years our school has gone from Special Measures, to Serious Weaknesses and finally to what is known by the Local Education Authority as a Category 3 school; thus requiring minimal supervision on their part.' (P 1)

'Raising attainment levels (as measured by SATs results) is the final hurdle we as a school have failed to leap and understandably it is seen to be the most important one – hence much attention and energy are directed towards this goal. ....throughout 2001 and 2002 much was put in place to try and raise standards, such as extended writing periods outside the Literacy Hour, plus time was set aside for cross-curricular writing in the Humanities. However, this was not reflected in the SATs results of 2002, with students still achieving 50% lower grades for their writing and their reading.' (P 2)

'Nationally in 2002 60% of children were gaining Level 4 in their SATs in writing (2% up on the previous year), little has changed over the past five years; see Table 1 below.

🕐 1999	2000	2001	2002	2003
56	55	58	60	60

Table 1 National percentage of Year 6 children attaining Level 4 in writing in the years 1999 – 2003   (P 6)

'Hypothesis'

Given what I have said in the introduction, I suggest that sustained exposure to and a confident knowledge of specific assessment criteria will raise individual writing standards in a Year 6 setting ......

It has been suggested in discussion that perhaps requiring Level 4 writing abilities of all 10 year olds, that is...

"...the ability to use writing for different purposes, to engage the reader, to structure a piece, to have some control over style and to conform to the conventions of grammar, spelling and handwriting..."
Sainsbury and Brill, 2003

is excessive with respect to a finite capacity processor and dependent on the automaticity of skills such as spelling and handwriting. However, if one limits the scope of skill to Wilson's four identified strands – vocabulary, connectives, openers and punctuation (or four generic targets as they are also called) – which

subsume all written genres, then perhaps it can be argued that the processing load is lightened as the spotlight of attention is focussed.

Prior to the introduction of Wilson's VCOP targets in my school, children and many teachers were ignorant of what separated a Level 4A piece of writing from a 4B, now with Wilson's Criterion Scale for assessment against the four targets (see Appendix 1), it is not only simple to grade children's writing within all levels, it is also simple to set targets for improvement – based on VCOP. In addition to this, these achievable targets can be couched in child-friendly language and exemplified with ease. Thus the children are enabled as learners to take control of and responsibility for their own improvement and even generate their own targets using the Criterion Scale.'(Pp 12/13)

'In summary my research questions are – will focussed teaching and modelling of Wilson's four strands and criterion level:

1. Lead to an increase in writing levels between baseline scores taken before the introduction of Wilson's scale and SATs scores attained in May, above those expected and greater than those in a group not involved in the intervention?

2. Result in a rise in the children's confidence in themselves as writers and enjoyment of writing as assessed through discussion and a five-point pictorial questionnaire?

3. Will these improvements be sustained into Year 7?'
(P 14)

Pupil interviews held in March 2003:

"Now I actually know exactly how and with what to improve my writing. Before I knew it wasn't good, but apart from copying from books I was reading I didn't know what to do..." **(Average Ability)**

"I used to get grumpy when you said we were going to do some writing, now I get excited because I want to see if I can earn group points for my work."
(Below Average Ability)

"I used to keep my writing private before because I did not want anyone but you to read it, but now I enjoy trying to use more openers and connectives than my SP and we try to beat each other with the number of ambitious words we put in our writing, by using the Thesaurus."
(Above Average Ability) (Pp 32/33)

Both the experimental and the control group were interviewed the week before the May tests:

'The experimental group were very animated and felt their writing had improved a great deal....

"I feel like a teacher sometimes now because I can look at my friend's work and tell her what level she is working at in VCOP."
(Above Average Ability)

In contrast the control group appeared subdued and concerned about their upcoming examinations.'
(P 35)

….all the children participating in the study made progress in their writing over the four month period that they were monitored, however… the experimental group made much greater gains.'
(P 38)

Of the 2 groups of 6 children;

In the experimental group pupils attained:

January 2003	May 2003	Value Added Sub-levels
3a	5	+4
3a	4b	+2
3c	4c	+3
3c	3a	+2
2b	3b	+3
2b	3b	+3

In the control group pupils attained:

January 2003	May 2003	Value Added Sub-levels
3a	4b	+2
3a	4c	+1
3c	4c	+3
3c	3a	+2
2b	2a	+1
2b	3c	+2

'Were the aims met?

(1) and (3) Yes the children's writing levels did increase between the baseline scores in March and the children's SAT results in May above that expected nationally and this rise was greater in the experimental group….. For it to be sustained however, it appears the programme of focused teaching methods needs to continue through the transition phase into secondary school.

(2) All the children except one in the control group reported through their responses to the questionnaire that their confidence level, enjoyment and attitude to writing had improved – the greater rating improvement was evidenced in the e.g., (experimental group), again supporting the aim.' (P 52)

'The Way Forward…

As the Literacy Co-ordinator I recognised the potential of Wilson's programme and thus organised an Inset for our school's staff with Ros. Wilson in September 2003. As a result of our borough-wide focus on raising standards in writing and our membership of an Education Action Zone pod we also invited all other member schools to join us. The day was a resounding success and all who attended were incredibly enthusiastic about the approach and set off to initiate it in their own schools.

….Now all classes in our two-form entry school use VCOP. Our results in this year's SATs I believe reflect these newly adopted focused teaching practices. OVER A TWO YEAR PERIOD WE HAVE GONE FROM 36% TO 55% AND NOW TO 72% LEVEL 4 IN LITERACY (I received the results only yesterday). In addition this year we have thirteen Level 5s in writing as opposed to four last year.'
(P 54)

Janine Ryan
September 2004

Key Stage Test Results 2004 – All Pupils
Percentage of Pupils achieving level 4 and above
2000 – 2004

📋 TEST	2000	2001	2002	2003	2004
English	56	56	37	55	73
Reading	67	65	46	59	75
Writing	37	40	25	24	61

(Adapted from school's PANDA 2004)

Hope X was formerly a pupil at Gainsborough Primary School. In May 2003 she completed the Year 5 Optional SATs, which were externally marked for Gainsborough Primary School. Hope was awarded a 3c for writing by the external marking.

The samples of work on the facing pages track Hope's progress throughout the Spring Term of 2004 as she works towards the taking of the national Year 6 tests. The reader can track Hope's progress as she moves from a level 3 in January 2004 to a Level 4 in April 2004. Hope was awarded a Level 4a for writing by the external SAT markers in May 2004.

See Hope's writing samples on the following pages.

Sample 1

Hope X
January 2004.
Gainsborough Primary

P

① Work on using dialogue Nora.

※ (Groaning) "Emily, Emily where are you!"
"It's okay I'm here, what happend to you!"
"I caught Mr. Hampton and his workers
digging under the ground to hind the stolen
gold, then bam! Someone hit me on my
head!" &
"Can you rember anything that happend?"
"No, I can't rember anythin' else, I didn't
mean to couse any trouble!"(Sobbing)
"Is that Cassandra, your friend?"
"Yes, It is!"
※ (She gasps) "He, He is the one that attacked
me as I was watching!"
※ (Shocked) "Tugger, How could you, I thought I could
trust you! What kind of friend are you?"
※ (Crying) "I, I thought she was a spyer!"
※ (Digging in distance) When you he hit on the head
a man or woman too put in this cave! I just
wissh I could go home, we should had never came
here! Emily, we could think of a plan to get
out!"
(Cheerfully) "Yes, we could if we do team work!
Tugger, sorry for overeacting before, I was just
shocked!"
"Don't I'll still help find a way out!

Sample 2.

The Magic Brush

Hope X
February 2004
Gavisborough Primary

Long ago, in a poor country in France there lived a
little girl called Lucian, (who) lived with a her parents.
Lucian loved to paint, although she was too poor to
afford a brush, she painted with a bunch of twigs
and or a sharp stone on walls. The poor little
girl worked from day to night to earn money to
feed her family.

One night as Lucian was sleeping a blaze of
light came and in came a fairy. She said "Here is
a magic brush, go into the village and help people."
Later on
The next day Lucian saw an elderly woman digging for
water with her hands. "You'll need a spade to dig." said
Lucian. Then drew a spade on the floor and it formed a
real spade.

Later on she saw a man walking for fifty miles and she
said "You'll need a horse to go," so she drew a horse
and then it formed to a real horse.
Finally, she saw people gathering for food, so she drew
a feast and everyone had food and drinks to eat.

The next day when she woke up she saw that people from
the next village had came to her village and
were complaining about them having food, water and
animals, because they didn't.
However However in the next village a Jealous
magician heard about it and soon made a plan to
kidnap Lucian.
After Lucian had finished school, the magician followed
her into a tunnel which had no light inside,

So Lucian drew a lamp. Suddenly as she turned around she saw a shadow behind her, but she just ~~sou~~ ~~conut~~ continued her walk. As she approached the end of the tunnel she heard footsteps and looked back and saw. ~~and saw~~ Dr. Evil (the magician) behind her. He quickly took a sack and put her inside, he ran past markets and gangsters to and finally into his ~~A~~ hixdting place - the cave. When he reached inside he threw Lucian in a cage and locked her in. Poor Lucian struggled to get out but it was no use! "Let me out, you kid stealer!" shouted Lucian. *

"You want to get out then, give me the magic brush = said Dr. evil nastily.
"Fine, I'll just stay here!" Lucian said angrily.
"Okay, you will have to draw me zis a chest full of gold, jewelly, crowns and money" shouted dr. Evil. Instead she drew a chest of slugs and worms. "You, little brat I wanted gold." screamed Dr Evil Then she quickily drew a dense fog to escape, then a horse, the horse galloped miles away from the magician. Unfortunatly the evil magician had a horse and climed on it and chased ~~h~~ after her. So she quickly drew a ~~hole~~ into which ~~and~~ he fell ~~inside~~ soon no-one ever heard from him again (he was not missed).

Then she ran home and told everyone what happend. They lived happily ever keter.
Great use of V C OP! Nora!
Work on: 7, 10, 15, 16,
Vary sentence length, use questions.

Sample 3.

Sat's

Hope X
April 2004
Gainsborough Primary

The alarm rang breaking the silent of a free-zone room. I jumped up trying to forget about the test. I hoped it was a dream! As I was trying to get up I heard a couple of school kids laughing threw the window. My heart was pounding! and It was like I was it was trying to escape all the gibberish I was feeling.

Fearfully, I got up and went inside the shower, timidly poured icey-cold water on me to relax, but it wasn't enougth. Calmly, I got out and looked in the mirror where my reflection was looking at me worredly, but I just ignored my personal feelings.

Minutes later, I went in the kitch-en feeling a little hungry, I & peeped in the fridge looking for milk to give me energy for the day. Little did I know, my mum was waiting in the car to give me a lift to school. I drunk the milk with one great big gulp and dashed outside to meet mum.

"I hope you're keen and up for the tests?" said mum, with a giggle.

It made me feel even angryer

HOPES WRITING **SAMPLE 3 cont**

than ever.

~~Later on,~~ As, we, reached the school gates I saw william my ~~&~~ classmate, who was sitting on the field feeling sorry for him-self. Swiftly, I kissed mum and ran out off the car, running to william to ~~And~~ disscuss the test.

"I think I might drop levels as I did last year," sobed William.

"Don't worry," I said in a friendly voice towards william.

"Maybe we should just chill out and have confidence in ourselves," he said.
Minutes later, the school bell rang, William and I hoped our teacher would be sick, instead she hopped along to ~~get~~ fetch us!
Oh, no, murmed other children, despite the fact they would still have to face the tests. We all ~~go~~ marched ~~down~~ the stairs to our classrooms, Finding the tables in two long rows ready for the day.

"As soon as you get your tests write your names & date on it!"

Suddenly, there was a large and loud knock on the door.

"Saved by the bell" I thought but it was the teacher Assitant coming to take some of the stupid people, including 'BILLY BULLY' to the libary ~~for~~ as they have 'extra needs'.
Unfortunately, it was ~~too~~ too late for me to act against the tests as Ms. Lucy was handing them out. She reached my desk and told me to do my best, so that I don't drop levels again, some people started giggling at the back of the room.

"I was more ~~litle~~ likely, to have a better level than Billy," I thought.

"You have & thirty-five minutes for the test, you're time starts now!", shouted Ms. Lucy.

Ten minutes has gone past and I'm still on question two when everyone was on question five. My legs ~~were~~ are ~~Sk~~ shaking and my heart is pounding really fast. Sweats ~~dripping~~ dripping from my face.

CASE STUDY 6
POPLAR PARTNERSHIP ACTION ZONE

Anna Burt, Zone Manager and Primary Co-ordinator for the Poplar Partnership Action Zone in the East 14 area of London, organised 'Big Writing' INSET for the schools in her zone on the 28th January 2005. This was requested and hosted by the head teacher and staff of Manorfield Primary School.

She has kindly provided the following, which are the collation of ALL the recorded comments on the evaluations completed by delegates.

Poplar Partnership Action Zone
Ros Wilson INSET on 28.1.05: Staff Evaluation

General

- I thought I had high expectations....this has taken them up another notch. Inspirational and entertaining! (Assistant Head – Mayflower)
- Absolutely brilliant afternoon. I will be confident about working on the Big Writing day with the tips and tricks learnt today. Great to have a speaker in education who is vibrant, exciting and fun.
- Very inspiring ; student work examples helpful
- Very inspiring ; good regarding Inclusion (SENCO)
- Didn't touch on drama before writing which was in the last INSET and I found very helpful
- Really liked the sound, clear, practical process for teaching writing
- Great day. Very interesting. Went fast with the humour
- Enjoyed the day. A lot to take away and think about/implement
- Very inspiring. Can't wait to start
- I am looking forward to implementing this in class
- Loved it all. Thanks very much. The children will benefit greatly from today. Keep driving around lots and enjoying your wine after work – you have heaps of great ideas!!
- An inspiring day. Just what I needed when the thought of being a Yr 6 teacher was becoming daunting. I'm going to go back and put it into practice
- A fantastic day – just as you suggested at the start of the day I'm eager to try this out in my classroom. I'm hoping writing will no longer be like drawing blood!
- Very motivating and inspiring. Can't wait to use all we learnt today in class. Thank you. PS Enjoyed your sense of humour!

CASE STUDY 7
ALL SAINTS' PRIMARY SCHOOL
ISLE OF WIGHT

Sallie Boulter is a Year 1/2 (mixed – age class) teacher in the above school. Her school participated in the Carisbrooke Cluster of Schools' Writing Project, 2003 to 2004, and it was through feedback from the cluster's Lead Teachers that her outstanding work came to our attention.

The facing pages show the Tracker Sallie maintained throughout the academic year, during which almost all 30 pupils moved from Level W or W+ to Level 2 or above. There is, included, an example of one pupil's initial baseline and final assessment to illustrate the progress reported.

Sallie is a talented teacher, and her testimony shows the wide range of strategies and the hard work that she put in to support her work in 'Big Writing' and in re-motivating and managing an initially challenging class.

This is Sallie's report on her work:

"I acquired my new Year 1 / 2 class in September 2003, made up of two groups from the previous Reception Class and Year 1.

I knew there were problems as the children's baseline profiles indicated low scores in the area of personal, social and emotional development. Many of these children had taken part in the school's specialist speech and language programme and despite the best efforts of a very experienced Early Years' Team, remained problematic in this area.

I knew it was going to be difficult to make significant progress with these children because they had poor interpersonal relationships. Included in this class were two children with very specific problems, one on the ADHD spectrum and one with severe emotional problems.

We spent the Autumn Term desperately trying to get to know each other and learning to work together as a class. A lot of time was spent on Circle Time. This was the primary focus of our attention.

It took me a long time to come to terms with the fact that hearing reading had to take a back seat for a while, yet I knew something had to go on hold for a while and if it had to be reading, so be it. Prioritising personal, social and emotional development was paramount.

The whole school had taken on the Ros. Wilson writing project, as we knew that writing was an area that needed attention. We had improved SAT results in every area except writing. We were willing to try anything –

especially a project that came with such good evidence of success and a very committed presenter!

So we got our package and off we went with VCOP (Very Clever Old People!). It took a lot of perseverance and patience with a class such as mine. I tried hard to make the sessions fast, fun, lively and pacey. We made a 'VCOP' wall and we all thought of exciting words to display.
We practised our handwriting religiously and we became adept at 'openers' (especially 'One snowy night....!) I taught the use of connectives by modelling. The children began to use them confidently. We knew the Punctuation Pyramid off by heart, and gradually we began to understand about full stops, capital letters etcetera and to use them appropriately.

Our first piece of Ros. Wilson writing in the September of that year was to be the baseline for the year's progress. As a class we all started somewhere along the 'W' spectrum. Our next piece in November was marked with anticipation. What if no progress had been made? However, this was not to be! Hooray! We had improved and this improvement continued throughout the year with some children moving from W+ to 2A in the 11 months. Not all the class made such fantastic progress but everyone did make progress at their own pace.

We worked on Basic Skills daily, especially high frequency words and handwriting. Thank heaven for individual whiteboards and pens! We even worked out a system whereby monitors could give resources and tools out in a calm and orderly way – a major breakthrough for my class.

Daily phonics teaching was in place in the literacy hour and children responded well to this. We had weekly spelling tests, which were written in silence – another major breakthrough for my children.

We had a rule that every child had the right to learn so any child that prevented this had a choice – sit, listen and contribute sensibly or leave the room. This worked well and by the second term I was able to reintroduce individual reading in the afternoons. By now I was beginning to relax and enjoy my class!

Puppets were popular so we used these for different aspects of 'VCOP'. We did stocking fillers, shared reading, shared writing and lots of modelling. I also introduced hot seating, which proved very popular and taught 'turn taking'. 'Big Writing' had a high profile each week, with classical music playing and candles creating a special atmosphere. By the end of the year we could all sit and write quietly and we had raised standards too! What an achievement!"

I feel that adopting the 'Big Writing' approach across the school enabled all colleagues to have a shared goal. We pulled together as a team, sharing ideas and successes. Standards were raised across the school. In both my class and my Year 2 colleague's class our SATs results for 2004 were proof of the improvement. Our PANDA results soared from an E in writing in 2003 to an A in 2004. Perhaps more important has been the experience of seeing children work specifically towards criteria-based targets, develop self-esteem and confidence, and above all enjoy writing!

Sallie Boulter
Class Teacher (Yr 1/2) March 2005

ISLE OF WIGHT TRACKER **SAMPLE 1**

Name	Gender	DOB	Year Group	Sep-03	Nov-03	Mar-04	Jul-04	Prediction for July 04	Sept to Nov	Sept to March	Sept to July
Adam	M	26-Feb-98	1	W	1a	2c		1a/2b	4	5	Void
Bradley	M	26-May-97	2	W	1b	1a	1a	1b/2c	3	4	4
Anna	F	20-Nov-97	1	W-	1b	2c	2b	1a/2b	4	6	7
Hannah	F	10-Oct-97	1	W+	1a	2b	2a	2c/2b	3	5	6
Susie	F	15-Sep-97	1	W-	1b	1a	2c	1b/2c	4	5	6
Kathryn	F	18-May-98	1	W-	1c	1a	2b	1b1a	3	5	7
Callum	M	02-Apr-98	1	W+	1a	2c	2b	1a/2b	3	4	5
Polly	F	13-Sep-96	2	W+	1b	2b	2b	1a/2b	2	5	5
Rachel	F	24-Mar-98	1	W+	1a	2b	2a	2c/2a	3	5	6
Gemma	F	15-Feb-98	1	W+	1a	2b	2a	2c/2a	3	5	6
Kelly	F	08-Oct-96	2	W+	1b	2c	2b	1a/2b	2	4	5
Karen	F	16-Mar-98	1	W-	W	1b	2b	1b/1a	1	4	7
Jenni	F	09-Nov-97	1	W-	1c	2c	2c	1b/1a	3	6	6
Francesca	F	25-Nov-96	2	W	1b	2c	2b	1a/2c	3	5	6
Michelle	F	25-Oct-97	1	W+	1a	2b	2a	2c/2a	3	5	6
Daniel	M	01-Jan-97	2	W+	2c	2b	2b	1b/2a	4	5	5
Charlotte	F	04-Dec-96	2	W	1c	1b	1a	1b/1a	2	3	4
Steven	M	18-May-97	2	W	1b	2c	2c	1c/2c	3	5	5
James	M	09-Jun-97	2	W	W	1c	1c	w/1c		2	2
Matthew	M	14-Oct-97	1	W	1a	2c	2b	2c/2a	4	5	6
Andrew	M	12-Jul-97	2	W	W	1b	2c	1c/1b		3	5
Dean	M	06-Feb-98	1	W-	1a	2c		1b/2b	5	6	Void
Ian	M	07-Mar-98	1	W-	W	1b		1c/1b	1	4	Void
Simon	M						1a			n.a	n.a
Charlotte	F						1a			n.a	n.a

EXEMPLIFICATION OF ONE CHILD'S PROGRESS FROM SEPTEMBER 2003 TO MAY 2004, 'MICHELLE' ON THE TRACKER. (Names have been changed to protect the children).

SAMPLE 1: September 2003

name: Sinead   W+   date: 25/7/03

Oen day
Ben and Tom
W'aet on a
maugc Toump and
fowy so~~mmmm~~ a poumsse
princess

SAMPLE 2: July 2004

Sinead (2A)

The Fly by Night

When the little girl who was called
Rosie was half way throoer the wood
she saw a little tiny fox. It was talking
Rosie said what is the matter ive lost my
home Ive lost mine to said Rosie.
We can help each other fund are home. Thats
a good idea said the fox Rosie said whats
your name the ~~fox~~ fox my mummy fox
didn't give me a name shull I give you
a name yes please he said why don't
I call you cuddly oh yes that a perfect
name. When. ~~were~~ Rosie saw three path to follow
but Rosie wanted to take the first path cuddly
wanted to take the last path they went and
folowed there own path and found there
proper home. When Rosie got hor

CASE STUDY 8
GRAVENEY PRIMARY SCHOOL, KENT

Graveney Primary School, is a small, rural school on the coast of Kent. The school had prioritised a need to raise standards in writing, and received one day's INSET on 'Big Writing' on the 17th November 2004.

On the 7th march, 2005, the Head teacher, Jane Troth, wrote to say how pleased she was with the progress made by pupils doing 'Big Writing' and included evidence from several pupils. Furthermore, she reported that children had complained when they had to miss 'Big Writing' to attend the pantomime at Christmas!

Two case studies are provided below.

Jane Troth says in her accompanying letter;

"Hopefully you will see from the November baseline what a positive impact your INSET has had on standards in a relatively short time!"

The following are examples of the amazing progress pupils in Key Stage 1 made in just two months:

Child 1: Jamie, Year 1, Level W+ to Level 2c

SAMPLE 1: Jamie, Year 1, 14.11.04, Level W

baseline   Year 1.

Sample 1   Jamie, Year 1
14.11.04 W+ →

W

Jamie 14.11.04

One bay Emily Wet to the Dot anb they Was a Dog anb Emily run at anb his run anb run fus anb they Was a Dog run anb run anb caB cum Duck fog anb they Was nun cuf they anb was suc they Was. anb he go hom Did cum

anb We cum Back

Jamie 26.11.04 Getting Reale P.E. Wt
ans tip 1. Getting you P.E. Cich.
2. ab Went you put you tip at
3. the PoPl ab We wil Be
4. Qiyt wenb the tich say
5. You con gau ing in the
6. hal ab sit Dayn no the
7. fol anb Be qut anb Say
8. uP ab hop We wil Be
SeBe inb are go to Play
9. in. Sus oom anb Sob

Sample 2 Jamie Year 1
26.11.04 Wt →

SAMPLE 3: Jamie, Year 1, 10.12.04

Sample 3 Jamie Year 1
10·12·04 Level 1c

Jamie Howard 10·12·04

one morning in class was nos

and miss Potts can hip the

chilon can hur miss Potts

Dot Do that! theywert at too a Play

ine. theay was rotee at play time

theay plad wic snowBall Gosle Smith

ted miss Potts miss Potts was hap

fereemuch miss Potts sed hood

plu Boke the wid Bel miss Pott

s.

14-1-05   Sample 4, Jarvie, 1a 1b/a

JaMie HoWaRD 14.1.05 LitLe ReT RiTiNgHooT

Once UP on LitLe Ret Ret Riding HooT

Went up sep sel and get her casx to go

to go her granTma Was PoTee. She Whs

vent in the Duc WOOS andso She WeRt

from the Duc DIP anT DUC WOOS.

She WaT littln Litle Ret RIDINgHo

WT. She got # they in time

She noTt on the Dor the GranTma

Was goT uP the GranTma Tea WaT

In the WoF Nf tUMee LitLe ReT Riding HooT

the Tdress up LICK agranma.

Litle ReT RiTiNg Hoover can inta.

then nase the WOF goT litl ReaRT

DT RiTingHooT in the WoF tUMee.

the WooTcutSuP the WoF TA timee.

FacK you SeT the get and theonTlaT

ee ReT HOOW WeRt nomee.

SAMPLE 5: Jamie, Year 1, 28.01.05, Level 2c

Jamie H 28.1.05

Sample 5 Jamie Year 1
28.1.05 2c

Once Upon a time there were three bears.

mummy bears made some a Porridge.

MUMMY bears said theis porridge.

then they went in the woods.

then Goldiocks cam in too the

house Nex she said theis is too hot

Next he went too the Next porridge.

but it could Next he went too the his

Porridge. Next She went in the

Luvingroom. but the Frhschair but in was too

hared. Noxt she went on the second

chair it is too soft Next she sat on baby

bear chair it has broc up in too little

Pisis. After she went upstairs she lad on the

bed she said itheis is too hot After she lad

on the second bed but it is too soft

After she went on the second bed

but it was Just right.

Child 2: Lexine, Year 2, Level 1b to Level 2b

SAMPLE 1: Lexi, Year 2, 26.11.04, Level 1

26.11.04

Lexi Year 2 Sample 1
26-11-04 Level 1

Lexi

Statt of school

First put you'r (your) Luch
Boocks (b) and yoo'r Boock (b)
bag on the bench.

↓

Next you whot for
the wissue to be ~~blon~~
blown and Line up
att your Line.

↓

~~T~~hen you what
~~a~~ for your techer
to say you are
alawd to go in.

SAMPLE 1continued: Lexi, Year 2, 26.11.04, Level 1

F
~~finle~~ you
go is your
class and
sit down on
the ~~tiplit~~ carpet.

Nekt you put
your Luch Boocks
one your peg.

Lexine   28.1.05

Lexi Year 2
Sample 2
Level 2B.
28.1.05

Once upon a time there lived
three bears. The first bear
was daddy bear the secsond
bear was mummy bear and there
was baby bear. They lived in a
small cottage. One day mummy
bear made some porridge but
it was too hot so they went
out for a walk. Then goldilocks
came and walked in the
small cottage. She tried
the big bowl of porridge. she
said "This is too hot!" After
she tried mummy bear's
porridge but that was
too sweet so she tried baby

CASE STUDY 9
'ROTHERHITHE WRITERS'

'Rotherhithe Writers' is a magazine for the children, parents, friends and staff of Rotherhithe Primary School in south east London.

The following contribution by Jasmine Dower is an excellent example of teacher's use of the resources in 'Strategies for Immediate Impact on Writing Standards':

Volume 1, Issue 1	Page 3

'Howl' by Jasmine Dower

Class 2 read an extract by Ros Wilson entitled 'Howl'. They were then asked to continue the story, writing the climax and resolution to the story in a similar style to the build up. Below is an excellent piece of writing by Jasmine Dower. Once you have read the story , you may want to see if you can spot 10 'wow' words that Jasmine has used.

Remember...

GOOD WRITERS CHOOSE THEIR WORDS CAREFULLY!

Eventually I pulled myself together and I began to do the job I had been sent there to do. Tugging sharply, I was able to budge the door enough for me to fit through. But a daunting sight met my big green eyes... the sight of stairs, stairs and more stairs. The shining marble surface of the stairs had traces of hair— hair which belonged to the Mangee.

After a while of padding up the great marble stairs, I paused to take a breather and that is when it happened... That is when I received the morale-booster I needed. The scream of the Mangee. It pulse through my veins. I cantered up the next 10 flights of stairs to meet my fate; The door to the dreaded bell tower. The gleaming door handle had an engraving which read

"Rivals of the heir BEWARE!"

Soon after, I was released from my spellbound state of mind. So I turned the handle of horror and pushed. I was ready. I turned my head in the direction of the now whimpering Mangee. The bear—like human was crouched in the corner. Next to him was the head of the temple with two deep lacerations to his chest... He was dead.

As I recovered from shock, it began— the mother of all fights. The Mangee sprang towards me. I dodged. But only just. Demented, it tried again and this time its aim was true, directly in my leg. I screamed, it howled and then he spoke,

"You are going to die!"

"Are you sure about that?" I quickly replied, as I pulled the glimmering dagger from my belt. Suddenly, I lunged and the dagger pierced its hairy chest. My foe, their foe, everyone's foe, finally dead. At last I had completed my mission!

Vocabulary Focus

Make a list of List some of the best descriptive words (the 'wow' words) Jasmine has used. ..

1._____

2._____

3._____

4._____

5._____

6._____

7._____

8._____

9._____

10._____

Next time you write a story, try to use some of these words.

GOOD LUCK!

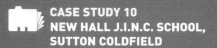

CASE STUDY 10
NEW HALL J.I.N.C. SCHOOL,
SUTTON COLDFIELD

New Hall Junior, Infant and Nursery Community School is situated on the Falcon Lodge estate on the outskirts of Sutton Coldfield. It is on a split site with the two sites being approximately half a mile apart.

New Hall J.I.N.C. School was in Special Measures until HMI recommended that they proceeded to their Section 10 inspection in February 2004. One of the final areas HMI had identified for improvement was to raise standards in writing.

The school received INSET on 'Big Writing' on Saturday, January 10th 2004. A Saturday was identified as the consultant could not otherwise address their need prior to HMI's return. Even so, she felt that the eight weeks between the INSET and his planned revisit was probably not sufficient to allow a positive enough impact.

The Head teacher and staff embraced the programme with enthusiasm. They had completed a baseline assessment for every pupil in the school in December of 2003, at the request of the consultant. They now taught VCOP and Basic Skills with vigour and then completed a second assessment prior to the HMI visit and updated their portfolio of evidence.

When HMI studied the school's evidence base and observed 'Big Writing' lessons he recommended them for their Section 10 inspection to take them out of Special Measures. In addition, he has since suggested to other schools struggling with writing, that they should visit New Hall and observe 'Big Writing' in practice.

Anna Jaremko (Literacy Co-ordinator and Year 4 teacher) and Heather Hudson, (Year 2 teacher and Key Stage 1 Literacy Co-ordinator) are now providing presentations for visiting teachers. The following are excerpts from their presentation;

"With a whole school approach, we soon found that not only were levels of attainment improving in writing, but that the children were approaching their writing with enthusiasm and enjoyment.

With this new initiative in place, our SATs results at both Key Stages 1 and 2 showed a dramatic improvement....

In last year's writing, an HMI area for concern, we had 28% of our children gaining Level 4 or above. We have increased this to 65% this year. Due to the implementation of 'Big Writing' and staff's enthusiasm and teaching we have managed a 37% increase in New Hall's writing standards. The number of level 5 writers has also risen by 17% to 19%.

Overall, English results at New Hall have improved by 22% to 79% at Level 4.

One year on and we are fully versed in 'Big Writing', our children are still enthused and our results keep improving."

The following are excerpts from the OFSTED report that confirmed New Hall J.I.N.C. School's removal from Special Measures:

EXCERPTS FROM NEW HALL J.I.N.C. SCHOOL'S OFSTED REPORT

SUMMER 2004

- At the end of Year 2 and Year 6, standards in English are below the levels expected for the pupils' ages largely because of weaknesses in writing. However, the recent introduction of a new approach to teaching writing is already having an effect on the quality and standards of the pupils' written work in literacy lessons and other subjects. The pupils have developed greater insight into the use of vocabulary, connectives, openings and punctuation as tools to improve the quality of expression. They are becoming enthusiastic writers and, in a very short period, there is evidence of improved standards in all year groups. A very high number of pupils in Year 6 have moved up one or more sub-levels within two months and many have already achieved or exceeded the targets set for them.

- In English and mathematics lessons, the pupils enjoyed discovering unknown facts and spontaneously celebrated insights shown by others. The consistent emphasis being given to using ambitious vocabulary or 'wow' words frequently elicited genuine wonder and excitement.

- In a Year 3 English lesson, the teacher's enjoyment and enthusiasm for the subject was transferred to the pupils through the lively and imaginative way in which explanations and instructions were given. The pupils lapped up new vocabulary and thrived on the challenge offered.

- As a result of recent in-service training, the school has successfully implemented a system called 'Big Writing'. This entails an intensive focus on extending the pupils' use of vocabulary, connectives, openings and punctuation to enable them to improve the quality of their writing. The teachers and pupils have taken to this with marked enthusiasm. Each week, a session of uninterrupted time for the pupils to apply their skills on an extended piece of writing is an integral part of the curriculum.

CASE STUDY 11
WILSDEN PRIMARY SCHOOL

Marie Blakely is a Year 6 teacher, Leading Literacy Teacher and Advanced Skills Teacher in Wilsden Primary School, a small rural primary school in a village setting outside Bingley, in West Yorkshire.

Marie provided the following Case Study, which is testimony to the hard work of the staff and includes excerpts from the school's OFSTED report.

"In the autumn term of 2003, 'Strategies for Immediate Impact on Writing Standards' arrived in school. A period of study followed in which I got my head around the principles and ideas within the text, the ideas of VCOP. I was motivated by what I read and felt strongly that the ideas within would prove successful in raising standards in writing throughout my school.

I initially introduced the 'idea' of VCOP to my year 6 colleague who was immediately taken by it; he too could see the potential benefits for our children.

In November 2003, I introduced the principles to the rest of the teaching staff. During a two hour training session, I carefully informed the staff about VCOP and how, through using these four generic targets, standards of writing could improve. My main aim was to give the staff something concrete to build upon, something to assist them in improving writing

standards. Motivation, inspiration, enthusiasm and commitment were needed from them in order for this to work throughout school. The ideas were welcomed by the staff, this was greatly appreciated as often you worry about introducing 'another new idea'; but they could see in principle how it could work. As a whole school we decided to put VCOP into practice.

As soon as I read about VCOP I wanted to personalise it for our school, I wanted to create a character that was tangible, someone who could be recognised instantly, someone who represented great writing. This character evolved as 'The V.Cop' - a police officer 'cop'. (This idea came from the letters VCOP – Vocabulary, Connectives, Openers and Punctuation.) Not only was this a visual stimulus for the children, it also enabled us to have a hierarchy for promotions as the children improved their writing, moving up the ranks of the police force. Every child began at Constable being able to move up to Sergeant, Inspector etc as their writing improved.

This is "The V.Cop"
As a result of the staff meeting each classroom had a specific area allocated for displaying VCOP. I produced a wide selection of resources for display purposes which were bright and interesting; staff were then asked to 'order' the resources they required for their classroom displays, these were then mass produced to help ease their workload. Each classroom, from Foundation Stage to Year 6, very quickly inherited its own VCOP area which soon became well used and fully interactive.

VCOP display in a Year 1 classroom

VCOP displays in a Year 6 classroom

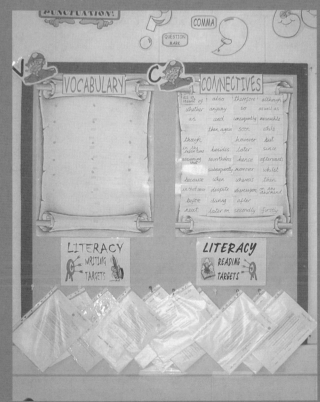

After informing the staff, I introduced VCOP to the children. My aim was to make writing more fun; I wanted them to be just as inspired as the staff were. In order to do this I lead two special assemblies using a PowerPoint. The V.Cop character was introduced and I explained in appropriate ways what each letter VCOP represented. The assembly ended with a song by Big Brovaz which includes the lyrics 'it ain't what you do it's the way that you do it... that's what gets results', this is now recognised throughout school as our V.Cop song! The children were dancing and having fun! They were motivated and excited by what they had seen and heard.

Throughout the months that followed, the staff put the principles of VCOP into practice; the children were incredibly responsive and increasingly more motivated to write. Children from Reception through to Year 6 were talking VCOP and were developing a sound understanding of how it could help them improve.

Each term, more regularly in Year 6, the children have a writing assessment. Their writing is marked and levelled using the Criterion Scale; targets are set from this also. It is, as a result of these assessments, that children can be promoted. The sense of excitement during promotions is fantastic! The children are very supportive of one another and are really inspired to achieve their new targets in as short a space of time as possible. Real excitement for writing comes from inspirational and positive staff; this definitely rubs off onto the children.

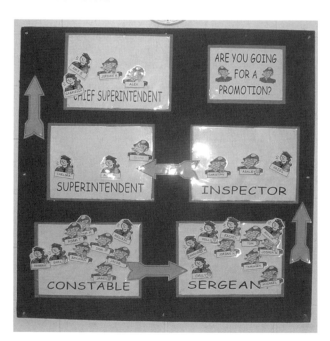

Are you going for promotion? Children in Key Stage 2 rise through the levels of the police ranks as their writing improves.

In May 2004, our school was subject to an OFSTED inspection. During this time the team were told about VCOP and the principles behind it; not just by me but also by the children. It was clear to the team, from the comments in their inspection report, that they too felt VCOP was beginning to make a difference to the standards of writing within school.

'The school is addressing the need to raise writing standards, most notably those of boys, partly through the recently introduced 'VCOP'... This is proving very effective and there are signs of raising standards with boys being more motivated in writing than previously.' (OFSTED inspection report May 2004)

The team also comment on how we involve the children in setting targets, encouraging them to take ownership of their achievements.

'Pupils are involved in monitoring their own progress through their individual targets. The recent introduction of the 'VCOP' monitoring system concentrating on the four generic targets is having a very significant effect on pupils' motivation to improve. It appeals particularly to the boys.'

'They are enthusiastically committed to using 'VCOP' as a strategy to check their own written work and make improvements.' (OFSTED inspection report May 2004)

Further comments from the report recognise how VCOP helps to boost the childrens' self-esteem.

'There is emphasis on pupil self-evaluation and improvement. The recently introduced 'VCOP' initiative is having a very positive impact on pupils' attitudes and learning.'

'...the group points system and, in particular the development of the 'VCOP' initiative, all make significant contributions to the promotion of pupils' development; these typify the teachers' enthusiasm and commitment.' (OFSTED inspection report May 2004)

After such positive comments from the OFSTED team, the way forward for school now is to ensure that VCOP stays alive and important to the children. (And indeed staff.) I regularly hold V.Cop assemblies, giving out certificates; playing our song and getting the children involved and excited once more helps to do this! I give staff ideas on how they can continue to excite the children. However, it is essential that each teacher develops an individual approach to delivering VCOP, something which is relevant to their children and suits their individual style of teaching."

Marie Blakeley
Wilsden Primary School, Bradford

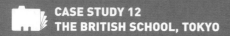

CASE STUDY 12
THE BRITISH SCHOOL, TOKYO

Background information

The British School in Tokyo (BST) is the only British School in the whole of Japan. We offer the programmes of study of the National Curriculum of England (2000) within the wonderfully diverse and rich cultural and physical context of Japan and East Asia. Our school is in the heart of Tokyo, one of the world's great cities. The learning opportunities are endless and our pupils benefit from a truly unique and memorable educational experience.

We currently have over 450 students on roll with the majority being of British nationality. Over 25 other nationalities are also represented within our student body, which ranges form 3 year olds, (nursery) through to 13 year olds (Year 8). All instruction, except in our Japanese and French language lessons, is in English.

Prior writing initiatives

Five years ago the school decided to fully implement the National Literacy Strategy from Years 1 – 6. This gave much needed structure and consistency of approach to the learning and teaching of literacy in these year groups. The turn-over of staff at BST, whilst not unusually high, is consistent and it was therefore thought that this initiative would provide a sound base from which to build the English curriculum.

Two mini inspections of the learning and teaching of Literacy were carried out in 2001 and 2002 by our then UK-based 'Critical Friend', a trained Ofsted inspector and LEA advisor. The input and guidance from this Critical Friend led to the implementation of child-speak writing targets across the school, regular literacy 'book looks and lesson looks' by the Head of Subject and English team, literacy boards in every classroom and Writing Wizards, a club for our very able and enthusiastic writers.

Our Key Stage 1 and Key Stage 2 National Curriculum Test results in English have been of a consistently good standard but there has always been a worryingly large gap between the achievement in reading and writing with standards in reading far exceeding those in writing. The raising of standards in writing was highlighted as a school development priority for the 2004 – 2005 academic year.

The Inset

Ros Wilson was engaged as our new Critical Friend with her priorities for focus being the raising of standards in writing along with the development of a more creative curriculum at BST. Ros became known to the school through her prior work with the current BST head teacher at another international school several years ago. The Director of Studies, having attended one of

Ros' one-day workshops in the UK on Raising Standards in Writing, recommended that this workshop be part of the 2004-2005 pre-school professional development programme for the whole staff.

Ros spent 3 days at BST in August, 2005. Having set the scene with thought-provoking examples of children's writing samples showing amazing leaps in progression, Ros introduced the staff to the concept of 'Big Writing'. The ethos of Big Writing tied in very nicely with the staff's desire to be able to approach the learning and teaching of literacy in general in a more creative manner. Whilst the rigour and thoroughness of the NLS was appreciated, it was also felt that teachers should now be able to have more autonomy and be free to be increasingly creative in their construction of learning opportunities for our students.

At BST, the 2004 – 2005 academic year has been the year of the Creative Curriculum. The advent of the Big Writing process in classrooms across the school has truly grabbed teachers' imagination and now, on a weekly basis, creative and original writing opportunities take place in each classroom.

Preparation for Implementation

Following the Inset in Tokyo on 'Raising Standards in Writing' the English curriculum team met with Ros to plan for the implementation of the Big Writing initiative at the British School in Tokyo. It was decided that one member of the team would lead the initiative and be responsible for managing the building of the children's portfolios, tracking the results of the writing assessments, organising peer coaching and supporting staff with the teaching of Big Writing throughout the year.

An Inset was delivered to staff to re-examine the theory and structure of Big Writing and to train teachers to use the strategies in lessons. This included further explanation of the four generic targets (VCOP) to ensure that this, and associated teaching strategies, would be adopted across the school. It also included ideas for creating a positive and stimulating writing environment in the classroom and examples of activities and scaffolds for writing.

I focused on developing an inspirational and exciting writing environment to motivate the children about Big Writing from the onset. I created and displayed connectives and openers word banks in my usual teaching space. The English team made punctuation pyramids for display in all classrooms and I made a bag of punctuation fans to hang in a bag on the wall in my writing area for easy access. I also created a 'WOW words' area of display with hanging stars and eye-catching slogans. The children add to this as an ongoing resource.

I developed 'Target Record Cards' for the children, based on Ros's examples in her book 'Strategies for Immediate Impact on Writing Standards'. These were shared with the children in earlier lessons to involve them in the writing assessment process. They are stored in their Big Writing folders to enable children to refer to them when completing writing tasks. They also allow the children to track their own progress in writing.

A Baseline Assessment Writing task was completed by all students at the beginning of the academic year. This was to ascertain children's initial writing levels to be used as the starting point for the tracking of children's progress in writing throughout the year and beyond. The children wrote a letter to the Head Teacher telling him about their summer holiday. The baseline tasks were levelled using the Criterion scale by the Director of Studies, Head of English, the Deputy Head Teacher and the Big Writing coordinator. Short term targets were set for each child. These targets were shared with the children using their piece of writing and the Target Record cards. The baseline assessments are stored in writing portfolios along with future writing assessments.

Introduction of Big Writing to the Children.
Each generic target was introduced in the first four Big Writing sessions of the school year. I have a large percentage of children in my Year Two class who have a kinaesthetic learning style so we developed a fun response to finding 'WOW' words in text! Children regularly tell me new 'WOW' words that they have learned. We play with them in class in oral activities to establish and reinforce meaning and the child then creates the word using 'Word-Art' to be displayed in the classroom. The punctuation pyramid was a hit and children were definitely motivated by being exposed to the levels. They immediately began to include more ambitious punctuation in their writing and were also able to identify a range of punctuation when reading. I was amazed that they were quickly able to use some level 4 punctuation marks. The ellipses were a strong favourite! The children and I quickly identified that they mostly used 'and' as a connective and enjoyed experimenting with other connectives and also openers to make their writing more interesting. There are endless activities that involve the children manipulating sentences and they enjoy playing with the word order and considering whether the meaning of the sentence changes. Again, these kinds of activities are especially valuable for kinaesthetic learners who are encouraged by tasks that do not initially entail writing. I have found that exposing the children to the examples of connectives and openers as much as possible has had a noticeable effect. They are displayed in the classroom, on their Target Record Cards and I also have connectives and openers cards which are useful for group or paired activities.

The children have a special Big Writing folder in which they keep their Target Record Cards, the writing completed during lessons and any stimulus material used as they are encouraged to 'steal' from others

writing. They will take this folder with them through the school and will serve as encouragement in how their writing skills are improving. Students enjoy the change in atmosphere during the Big Writing sessions. I burn a candle and essential oil to 'oil our writing brains', dim the lights and play Mozart. It is amazing how this creates such a calm and motivated atmosphere. The children now ask, "Shall I turn down the lights?" Of course, tiny cookies used as rewards are also a huge motivator! Big Writing sessions definitely have a different 'feel' to other lessons in the timetable. I think the two halves of the session really complement one another, the first part being fast, fun, kinaesthetic and mainly oral activities and the second part quiet, calm, sustained writing time. One of the obstacles I have often come up against in the past when teaching writing is having enough time to give an effective stimulus for writing ideas and giving children enough time to complete their writing. The extended structure of the Big Writing lesson allows me to do this. The children always feel a wonderful sense of achievement at the end of the session.

Ongoing Implementation and Results
I am currently in the process of organising the support of teachers with Big Writing across the school. Support is being offered in a number of ways:

1. Teachers observing myself and members of the English team/leading teachers in Big Writing teaching Big Writing
2. Teachers having an informal Big Writing lesson observation with me and then feedback to support teaching.
3. Myself and teachers planning and team teaching a Big Writing lesson to their class.
4. Planning a series of Big Writing lessons with year groups and then evaluating the success of the lesson when delivered.
5. I will be providing resource packs with activity ideas for teachers to use in their lessons.

Writing Progress Trackers
Initially, writing levels for each child are entered by hand onto a Writing Tracker. At this time a target level is recorded for the next term and one or two areas of writing highlighted for focus in order to move the child on in their writing.

In addition, every child's writing level is entered into the Writing Assessment database. From this database, each teacher is then provided with three documents:

• **Writing Assessment Progress Tracker:** provides a class overview of levels achieved over the course of the year and a visual indication by use of colour-coding of progress made;

• **Writing Assessment Progress by Class:** a horizontal bar-chart showing each child's progress compared to the other children in the class;

- **Individual Progress Graphs:** a vertical bar-chart for each child recording the result of each writing assessment in a different colour.

Each of the above documents has been gratefully received by staff. The documents clearly indicate which children are making good progress and which are not. Teachers are able to very easily identify those children who are in danger of either not progressing sufficiently or who are regressing, and plan writing lessons around this information.

Quick Impact Strategies course

After the first term of Big Writing at the British School, I attended the Quick Impact Strategies course in the UK. This involved analysing the four generic targets and examining strategies for quick impact upon children's writing. This was an excellent opportunity for me to refresh the knowledge that I had gathered during the three day training at the beginning of the school year. There were many more practical ideas for lessons and fillers during the day for teaching and reinforcing these essential skills. I could hardly wait to get back to Tokyo to try them! One of the best ideas that came from this session was the VCOP clock. This is a coloured clock used for timing prompts. The clock is divided into six 10 minutes segments: one for each generic target, one for full stops and capital letters (basic skill) and one for the child's personal writing target. I now use this clock as a tool for children to edit their own writing in every Big Writing session. I have used it as an aid to teach the children the importance of self editing their writing. In addition to ongoing editing, the children are also given ten minutes proof reading time where they are learning to analyse each sentence and try to improve it by adding some VCOP. The use of 'sparkly pens' is a good motivator in this activity!

Future Planning (Term 3)
- Involving Parents – presentation to parents about the Big Writing Initiative at the BST

- Training teachers to level writing using the Criterion Scale/organising agreement trialling

- Setting up a database interface on each teacher's class computer so as to facilitate easy and immediate access to every child's termly Writing Tasks achievements and progress.

 NB A COMPREHENSIVE RANGE OF ASSESSMENT MATERIALS PROVIDED BY THE BRITISH SCHOOL, TOKYO, HAS BEEN INCLUDED AS APPENDIX 6 AT THE BACK OF THIS PUBLICATION. IT INCLUDES A MODEL OF THE 6 QUICK IMPACT LESSON PLANS FROM 'STRATEGIES FOR IMMEDIATE IMPACT ON WRITING STANDARDS' ADAPTED FOR YEAR 2.

CASE STUDY 13
GLEBE JUNIOR SCHOOL, DERBYSHIRE

The writer has received considerable support from Janet Mort, a senior teacher at the above school. She has implemented the strategies throughout the school, with considerable success and has provided ongoing feedback and advice.

Janet provided further examples of generalising words, which have been included in the pupils' targets in Chapter 5. In addition, Janet co-ordinated the making of a video of teachers teaching 'Big Writing', which we now use on courses.

The following is an excerpt from recent feedback received from Janet:

"Archetypal Level 2c – 3b improvement

September Baseline: Task – introducing themselves to their new teacher

Dear Mrs. _____

In the six week holiday I was going near a lake to cachr some frogs. I court a big frog with my frends sometimes it got boring so we made some dens. When we have got frogs we take the to my frends house. The last week in the six week holiday   we see 11 fish and a warter snake.

I have 7 pets in my house 3 fish 2 dogs and 2 ginipigs I like my pets. I haft to feed mu pets   I cleen my fish tank out and the ginipig cages I give my dogs a bath.

The sport I like is football and I play for a football team. My team is called pinxton viler and I go to football training with my team the last football game we had was on sataday when we won 3-0 to us.

My best color is gold, my second is red I usely colour in red.

March Assessment: Task – Writing a letter to a friend who does not live in South Normanton about the night when strange lights headed towards the town / aliens landed.

Dear Jake,

One amazingly dark night, I woke up after spotting something in the skiy which looked like slugey green snow. Suddenly a space ship flow down onto the school grounds and landed inside our car park.. It was the most unbelievable thing I had ever seen!

After that the door busted open and some electric stairs descended. The spacecraft looked a dark dark thing but

I couldent tell from the distance we were apart. Amediately something came out of the spaceship and before long had broken all the fenses and had taken over South Normanton! A while later, I caught sight of the strange alians which were bright orange with triangler heads. After that the alians went back to there own spaceship and eventually returned to there very weyod planet.

I run up stirs and in the morning I told my mum and dad all about it but they simply dident belive a thing I said.

Love.............

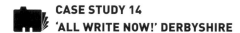

CASE STUDY 14
'ALL WRITE NOW!' DERBYSHIRE

Ian McCollum manages the **'ALL WRITE NOW'** project in Matlock, Derbyshire. He has skilfully adapted aspects of Big Writing to combine with the ideas of his own team in order to better help teachers and teaching assistants in the area. Some of the materials developed by Ian are included in the appendices.

Read On – Write Away! is an Independent Literacy Partnership based in Matlock, Derbyshire. Partners include Derbyshire County Council; Derby City Council; Derbyshire Learning & Skills Council; the Basic Skills Agency and the National Literacy Trust.

I'd been involved with ROWA for some years as a Better Reading Partnership trainer when, in 2000, I was offered a secondment to write a new 'Better Writing Partnership'. Eventually, this developed into 'Push On Writing' – a 2-day course for volunteers and Teaching Assistants who needed to motivate small groups of KS2/3 children [particularly boys] and provide ideas for creative writing.
Each participating school was expected to send a teacher coordinator on the second day of the course and it was encouraging comments from these teachers that made us start thinking about developing a whole-school writing strategy introduced through an INSET Day. Although 'Push on Writing!' is an effective motivational package for small group work it required an enormous amount of development to make it useful for teachers throughout Key Stages 1 and 2.

I collected together a team of serving teachers to explore ideas that would give the project a straightforward structure to complement the existing motivational elements. It was in 2002 that our research group came into contact with Ros Wilson's work. Within minutes, we realised that Ros had already done all the research and development hard work and the only thing we needed to do was to ask her permission to combine her strategies with Push On Writing! and our new material.

Ros was enormously generous with her time and support. Permission to use some of her ideas was granted and 'All Write Now!' was born.

After further developments to merge the projects into a cohesive strategy, we now believe we have the perfect combination of activities to promote writing in the primary school.

ROWA! is principally a community learning organisation and our aims were to create something that would involve whole families in writing. It also had to be fun for children and their teachers but should not increase teacher workload.

'All Write Now!' is based on the premise that improved speaking skill is the key to improved writing. We aim to raise each child's writing level closer to his/her speaking level at the same time as we bring the speaking level ever closer to the child's thinking level. Increasing each child's thinking processes through prepared discussion is intended to lead to a process of constant development.

All the resources are provided on CD.
Children are given targets to reach clearly defined writing goalposts. They are empowered to make judgements on the levels of their own and other people's writing. Self-assessment forms are included and children can be taught to analyse their own writing in terms of secretarial skills and, more subjectively, in interest level. Games provide the incentive for quick thinking – children learn how to make up a simple story in only a few seconds. Storytelling to audiences encourages confidence. Graded 'posh speak' exercises develop vocabulary and sentence construction. 'Telling Lies' is encouraged [under strictly controlled rules, of course]! Board games create discussion around punctuation and ambitious words. Children learn the arts of note-taking, story-boarding and basic mind-mapping to aid the creative processes.

We also promote the use of 'minibooks' – based on Paul Johnson's ideas. Children become 'authors' and their writing reaches a much wider audience than ever before. Years 5 and 6 are encouraged to provide one to one support to younger children in writing lessons. Discussing the quality of writing becomes a whole-school pastime!

Material explaining the strategy to parents is also included.

But it's Ros Wilson's 'Big Writing Day' structure that holds it all together! VCOP takes care of much of the requirement to learn secretarial skills and gives teachers a straightforward structure for teaching grammar in a way that children recognise as relevant. Increasingly interesting content is developed through cross-curricular discussion and modelling during lesson time.

In Foundation classes 'Big Talking Day' introduces the structure and skills children will need later to become enthusiastic writers.

The whole project fits seamlessly into schools using a thematic approach and requires little effort to apply to any curriculum subject. AWN! provides sample BWD modules for science, geography, history and RE.

Read On – Write Away! is deeply grateful to Ros Wilson for the consistent support and encouragement she has provided. We have evaluated all her strategies included in 'All Write Now!' and have found her claims to be entirely justified. Ros Wilson's strategies really do improve standards in writing!

I am delighted that Ros has felt able to promote some of the 'All Write Now!' teaching material. We are proud to be able to make a small contribution to her work in schools.

Ian McCollum
Training & Development Manager
Read On- Write Away!

Sue Beckett is Deputy Headteacher of Christchurch CE Primary School, Chesterfield. She is also a 'Push on Writing!' trainer for ROWA! and has been active in the development of 'All Write Now!'
Sue introduced the complete range of AWN! strategies into her Y1 & Y2 class in September 2004.

Sue says: "I love Big Writing Day. We have a quick look at the structure of the writing task – normally in stick-picture form – then we rehearse our first sentences to partners and we're away! We put on gentle music and relax as we enjoy putting our thoughts down on paper. Each week a 'star writer' is chosen for doing their best ever writing – this is often a difficult choice because the children are making such good progress."

Comments and levels from a cross section of Sue's class:

Jessica, Year 2, Sept. 04 = Level 1a, April 05 = Level 2b
"I love writing because it is fascinating, fun, adventurous and it is one of my favourite things."

Thomas, Year 1, Sept. 04 = Level 1a, April 05 = Level 2b
"I love writing because I like imagining things."

Courtney, Year 2, Sept. 04 = Level 1a, April 05 = Level 2b
"I love writing because I like the sparkling adventures in my books. I am happy in my books."

Sam, Year 1, Sept. 04 = Level 1a, April 05 = Level 2a
"I love writing because I use brilliant words. I write interesting stories, too."

Nate, Year 2, Sept. 04 = L W [low], April 05 = Level 2c
[resistant to writing] [happy writer]
"I love writing because I love using my imagination and interesting words."

Joshua, Year 2, Sept. 04 = Level 2c, April 05 = Level 3c
"I like thinking. I like my dark wood [story] because the phantom train saved me."

Sara, Year 1, Sept. 04 = L W [good], April 05 = Level 2b
"When you write stories it's lots of fun."

Luke, Year 1, Sept. 04 = Level 1b, April 05 = Level 2c
"It is funny to write letters and tell people funny stories."

Emma, Year 2, Sept. 04 = Level 2c, April 05 = Level 3
"I imagine that I am in the story."

Sue is about to reassess all the children as part of 2005 KS1 SATs. She estimates that most of the class will score at a sub-level higher than those shown above.

 NB A SELECTION OF RESOURCES AND ACTIVITIES PROVIDED BY IAN AND THE 'ALL WRITE NOW' TEAM IS PROVIDED IN APPENDIX 3 AT THE REAR OF THIS PUBLICATION.

CASE STUDY 15
LOVE LANE FIRST SCHOOL, ISLE OF WIGHT

Steve Bartlett is head teacher of Love Lane First School on the Isle of Wight. His excellent leadership of the introduction of Big Writing in his school, and the hard work of his talented team of teachers, support staff and pupils, has led to its great success. Steve has generously allowed us to publish his data.

Dear Ros,

Sorry about the delay, but here is the information demonstrating the progress made since October half term 2004.

I have included the overview data, the spreadsheets for all classes, and the information graphically. The two sets of graphs are the same, except one of them has our targets on them as well. (You probably will not want that information).

I will send this by post as well as e-mail.

I must point out that the Y2 results have been achieved following one disappointing term with a teacher who has since left us, (between October and December this class did very little which makes the results even more impressive) and then one term with an excellent replacement.

We are involved in a pilot project for KS2 linking our Y3/4 children with the middle schools Y5/6. Part of this involves a visit from an LEA consultant to talk to a sample of 10 children and to look at their work. Following our visit she was very complimentary.

Feel free to use any of the data in whatever way you want.

The Ros Wilson approach to writing has had a huge impact at Love Lane in terms of raising the standards of writing across the school, but more importantly in generating enthusiasm for writing amongst the staff and the children. We are on course to meet our targets and this should result in the removal of Serious Weakness.

Steve Bartlett

CASE STUDY 16
WEST DUNBARTONSHIRE, SCOTLAND

Agnes McGrogan is a highly experienced former head teacher currently working in the role of a Quality Improvement Officer for the education department of West Dunbartonshire Council. She has led a most impressive project on writing in her area, the outcomes of which will be published on its completion.

As part of this project, a team of expert assessors have adapted the Criterion Scale for use within the Scottish levels for writing, which are different from the English ones. This has been a great success with teachers in the locality as, like the Criterion Scale, it provides detailed small step criteria to support accurate assessment and inform targets.

Agnes has kindly given permission for its use and it is presented as Appendix 5 at the rear of this publication.

A local authority develops the 'Ros Wilson ' approach.

'Inspirational, Renewed Optimism, one of the most enjoyable and practical courses I have ever attended, all teachers MUST have this'

As Quality Improvement Officer with responsibility for the development literacy, a major part of my work involves organising training for staff. Having been approached by a secondary teacher to invite Ros to our area I proceeded to make the usual arrangements, not realising that there would be nothing 'usual' about what we were about to experience. The day duly arrived when we gathered to hear about this new approach to assessing pupils' writing and strategies to use when intervening to promote learning. After a very short time it became evident that there was something very special about both the presenter and her material.

The course participants were enthralled as they experienced a wonderful blend of humour and information on how to effect change in pupil performance. Never before had we received such overwhelmingly complimentary evaluations:

'I can't wait to get back to my class to try this out'
'She is so motivational she made me believe I can do this'
'Please don't let this be a one-off course we must take it forward in our local authority'

As a result West Dunbartonshire is currently running an authority-wide assessment project looking at standards of writing in P7 (Year 6 in England) – S1 (Year 7 in England). The aims of our project are:

- to use the criterion scale to develop an assessment tool for writing that has more detailed criteria than the current 5 -14 targets and which provides next steps for sharing with pupils.

- to gather information about strengths and areas of development of P7 and S1 pupils through assessing unsupported pieces of writing, and to use the information gained to inform learning and teaching in both sectors.

• to train staff from both sectors in using the criterion referenced assessment scale and to standardise marking.

Following the initial course a cross sectoral group was set up to begin adapting the criteria to suit the 5 -14 levels and provide sub-levels within each level thus giving an indication of low, middle or high performance at a specific level. Samples of pupils' work were then assessed to provide exemplars of each level. These were used to train markers who would be assessing the test pieces.

A great deal of interest amongst teachers from both primary and secondary sectors was generated and as a result some action research was undertaken using the criteria and investigating their effectiveness in diagnosing strengths and weaknesses in children's writing. In order to track progress, every P7 pupil from each of our 35 primaries did a short test of writing in June 2004, another piece in September (now in secondary 1) and a third piece in May 2005. Additionally two primaries were selected to trial the interventionist strategies which were readily embraced by teachers as relevant and practical.

It is already obvious that the use of more specific criteria highlights areas of strength and weakness, and this information will be very useful to schools for planning how to raise standards in writing. Feedback from the primaries involved in the intervention has been most encouraging with teachers commenting on the growing awareness of pupils' knowledge and understanding of key skills.

Further staff development is planned to reach all primary and secondary English teachers.

This comment made by a teacher of thirty years experience is typical of many.

'I want to tell everyone about this, people need to know that this will revolutionise their teaching and give them so much confidence. Children who loathed writing are asking when they are having their next writing lesson'.

West Dunbartonshire classrooms have never quite been the same since the formidable Ros came into town.

Julie Horsington is a newly qualified teacher currently teaching Year 6 at Southern Road Primary School.

Southern Road Primary School is a large, four form entry primary school in the Plaistow area of the London Borough of Newham. The current number on role is 868 of whom 68% have English as an additional language (EAL) 13% have special educational needs and over 50% are entitled to free school meals. There has been a dramatic rise in mobility in the academic years 2003/04 and 2004/05.

Julie writes:

"I first thought of Kung Fu punctuation when the literacy consultant for Newham, Pam. Clarke, came into my classroom to teach the 6 'quick impact'/'raising achievement' lessons from Ros. Wilson's book.

Although my pupils were only taught from this remarkable programme for a brief time period, the improvements made in their writing were astonishing. Not only did this programme raise standards in pupils' skills and writing but it also raised enthusiasm levels in my class due to the fun, stimulating nature of the activities Ros. has developed.

The development of Kung Fu punctuation really came from the pupils themselves. The energy and enthusiasm they displayed really carried this activity to the next level. This idea was a development from one of Ros.'s activities and is all about promoting the idea of learning being fun."

INSTRUCTIONS FOR PUNCTUATION KUNG FU

1. Refer to the Punctuation Pyramid on display in the classroom and review which punctuation marks the children should be using for their target levels. e.g. Do they know which they should be able to use at Level 3?

2. Teach the children the physical actions for the punctuation signs (see below).

3. Read out the first prepared sentence. e.g. Although Kathy knew that it was cheating, she could not help taking a peep.

4. Give the children 10 seconds thinking time to work out the punctuation for each sentence.

5. The teacher says, "First punctuation mark!"

6. Children respond, "HUH!" as they perform the action for a capital letter.

7. Teacher says, "Second punctuation mark!"

8. Children respond, "HUH!" as they perform the action for a comma. If the punctuation mark has two movements, as in an exclamation mark, children must say, "HUH! HUH!" as they perform the two movements.

9. Teacher says, "Third punctuation mark!"

10. Children respond "HUH!" as they perform the action for a full stop.

11. Briefly discuss any elements of usage felt necessary before going on to the next sentence.

THE PHYSICAL ACTIONS

NB EACH MOVEMENT MUST BE ACCOMPANIED BY A GUTTERAL "HUH!" AS IN THE SPORT, KUNG FU.

ALL PUPILS SHOULD STAND AND FACE THE TEACHER.

1. CAPITAL LETTER	Both hands above head, finger tips together and thumbs touching to form capital A shape.
2. FULL STOP.	Punch air forwards once, horizontally.
3. QUESTION MARK?	Right hand raised to make comma shape, left fist punches once sideways below.
4. EXCLAMATION MARK!	Right arm raised high, then dropped. Left fist punches once sideways below.
5. COMMA,	Right elbow at waist, with forearm pointing upwards, make 'hook' or comma shape at the top with right hand.
6. ELLIPSES...	3 horizontal forward punches
7. SPEECH MARKS ""	Arms raised, both hands form " to top left of body and then rapidly again to top right.
8. DASH -	Horizontal karate chop sideways with right hand, which is open and flat with palm downwards.

9. APOSTROPHE' Arm raised to form comma shape in the air above the head.

10. COLON: 2 horizontal punches forward, first one above the second one.

11. SEMI COLON; Right hand makes comma shape at chest height, left hand punches horizontally and sideways above it.

12. BRACKETS () Big curved shape with left arm extended upwards to left of head, followed by big curved shape with right arm extended upwards to right of head.

EXAMPLES OF SENTENCES USED WITH JULIE'S CLASS

1. This is a pencil.

2. Where is my phone?

3. Come here at once!

4. Have you seen my keys?

5. Harry woke up early the next morning.

6. Although he could tell it was daylight, he kept his eyes shut.

7. All of a sudden....

8. That's outrageous!

9. The sky was quite clear now and the sea gleamed in the sunlight.

10. Hagrid's coat seemed to be made of nothing but pockets, bunches of keys, slug pellets, balls of string, mint humbugs and tea bags.

An Additional Adaptation to Kung Fu Punctuation by the writer.

All pupils stand facing teacher with feet approximately one and a half feet/45 cms apart. They bend their knees slightly.

Pupils give TWO 'HUHs' for each piece of punctuation:

HUH 1: Small jump with bent knees
Right arm in front of chest bent at elbow with forearm pointing upwards, fingers together and pointed upwards
Left arm bent at elbow across chest beyond right arm, fingers together and pointing horizontally

HUH 2: Second small jump with bent knees
One or both arms making sign for punctuation as above.
There will be 3 'HUHs' if the piece of punctuation has 2 Moves.

Each time they shout "HUH!" for any movement they actually make a small jump with bent knees

ACTIVITY 1

OPEN TENNIS TOURNAMENTS

You will need:

Three, four, five or six players.
Openers and connectives fans

The teacher will pre-decide whether servers can only take the openers from one specific side of the fan, (L2/3 or L4/5) or from either.

Three or four players:

Two players take the 'ends' for Game 1, by sitting at each end of a table.

The third player sits half way along on one side and is the umpire. If four are playing there is an umpire each side.

The two active players have an opener and connective fan each.

The umpire has a stop watch.

The server calls out any of the words that can legitimately be used as an opener and the receiver has to immediately continue and complete a coherent sentence.

The umpire allows up to 3 seconds before the receiver must respond. The time is adjusted at the teacher's discretion.

The umpire judges, a) whether the opener was legitimate and b) whether the sentence is a complete and coherent one. If so the server has scored. If four are playing these two roles may be separated with each umpire taking one role.

The receiver now becomes the server and calls a new opener, which the previous server receives and uses to immediate create a new sentence.

Scoring may either be as in tennis, (15 love, 15 all etc) or as in ping pong, going up in ones to 21).

NB the umpire need not speak unless s/he detects an error either in opener or sentence, in which case s/he calls out 'Fault' and explains the judgement. The three may then debate the judgement if one of the players challenges it, and consult a 'professional' if necessary. 'Professionals' may be acknowledged class experts or adults.

Five or six players:

There are now two 'pairs', one at each end of the table. Pairs play on the same side and support each other in scoring.

Serves rotate round the table clockwise, so that each pair serves in turn. However, either of the receiving pair can fire back the sentence (peer support for differentiation). The first to speak provides the answer. This CAN be changed so that the diagonally opposite player MUST receive and complete.

There may be one or two umpires depending on whether five or six pupils are playing.

INCREASED CHALLENGE LEVEL

Challenge can be increased by the umpire calling out the subject/stimulus for the sentence BEFORE OR AFTER the server serves the opener.

 Example (3 players):

UMPIRE	Hobbies! *(Starts timer)*
SERVER 1	Despite
RECEIVER 1	Despite enjoying cycling, Deidre preferred to swim.
UMPIRE	*(Stops timer)* Love 15. The Queen. *(Starts timer)*
SERVER 2	Contrary to....
RECEIVER 2	*(Silent)*
UMPIRE	*(Stops timer)* Fault. Love 30. The Pennines

ACTIVITY 2

Scrambled sentences:

Make up sentences that model the language you are embedding for your children.

 Example

1. Regrettably our esteemed head teacher has decided to cancel the summer holiday, due to the intense pressures of the curriculum.

2. Doubting that students in this class are absorbing sufficient knowledge, I have determined that school will remain open seven days per week.

Scramble them, e.g:

1. decided cancel regrettably curriculum to to due our intense head teacher esteemed holiday pressures summer the of the has the

2. will determined doubting seven days that in absorbing class students I per this remain week knowledge open school this are sufficient have.

The first word of each sentence should be identified for pupils. It should normally be a connective, an 'ly' word or an 'ing' word to promote VCOP.

An extension can be to ask pupils to see how many different ways they can find for structuring the sentence, using only the words given.

 NB THERE IS OFTEN MORE THAN ONE WAY TO RE-ASSEMBLE A SENTENCE AND STILL MAINTAIN COHERENCE. A TEACHER MUST NOT ASSUME IT IS 'WRONG' IF IT DOES NOT MATCH THE ORIGINAL.

THE EXAMPLES ABOVE ARE TOO COMPLEX FOR THE INTRODUCTION OF THIS ACTIVITY. PUPILS NEED TO BE TAUGHT TO CLUSTER PHRASES AND USE THE CIRCLE STRATEGY TO CREATE SENSE (placing words in a circle).

PUPILS SHOULD BE GIVEN THE WORDS IN SHUFFLED SETS OF CARDS, AT LEAST INITIALLY, IN ORDER TO ENABLE THE CIRCLE STRATEGY AND TO ENABLE ACCESS FOR ALL LEARNING STYLES.

The following is a more appropriate introductory sentence:

> walking to school, I found a pound.
> found school I walking pound a to

Please note that this example has coherence implications. Pupils may structure it as, 'I found a pound walking to school.'

The implications for meaning will need to be discussed here, 'Was the pound walking to school?' 'Which other word would you have needed to make this sensible?' Also the connection to higher level sentences when opened with the 'ing' word.

In most cases pupils should be expected to open every sentence with a connective, 'ing' or 'ly' word and this would usually prevent the above error.

Having reassembled the sentence on the cards, pupils should record it on scrap paper, a personal whiteboard or the screen of a laptop or PC.

ACTIVITY 3

Scrambled Words

Use this to reinforce learning of words and spelling of key words for 'Big Writing' or for technical language in any subject.

 NB All words should already be familiar to the class.

 Example:

WORD 1	trepidation
WORD 2	delapidated
WORD 3	earthquake

Scrambled:

WORD 1	pdairnteiot
WORD 2	ddditealpae
WORD 3	qkaetehar

For each word, pupils should be given a clue. This may be a definition or reference to where the class recently met the word. For example, the teacher may say,

> "These are all 'wow' words we used in this week's 'Big Writing' lesson."

The teacher may also supply the initial letter at her/his discretion.

Pupils should be taught to put the letters in a circle to help with decoding.

Some pupils may benefit from having the letters on pieces of paper or post-its, particularly kinaesthetic learners.

ACTIVITY 5

Thesaurus Megasaurus

Each player has a thesaurus.

Game 1

Usually played in 2s, however less able pupils may be better with 2 other players (3s), if they find the use of a thesaurus hard.

Player 1 selects a word and gives two of the synonyms.

Player 2 has to guess what the word is OR give a third synonym.

Now Player 2 selects a word and game continues with players scoring one point for each correct guess. First to 5 (or up to 10) wins.

Game 2

Two players have closed copies of a thesaurus. Third has a stop watch and a thesaurus.

Third player finds and calls out a word and starts the stop watch.

Two players search for word against the clock.

First to find the word shouts it out and then reads the synonyms.

The player scores one point.

If neither has found the word within a prescribed time frame the third player must read out the word and synonyms, and s/he scores a point.

First to 5 (or up to10) wins.

Adapted Game 2

Use dictionaries and players call out definitions.

ACTIVITY 6

Super Spellers

3 Players

Player 1 has dictionary and stop watch. S/he finds a word and calls it out.

Two other players have personal white boards and markers. They write the word and show to Player 1.

First of the 2 players to show scores two points if word is spelled right.

If word is spelled wrong, second player scores one point providing her/his word is spelled correctly.

 NB Player 1 must be able to spell the word her/himself.

If a player thinks Player 1 may not be able to spell the word, they shout 'Challenge'.

Player 1 must now close the dictionary and spell the word. If s/he is able to s/he scores a bonus point.

If s/he is unable, the challenger scores a bonus point.

 NB This may be limited to words with regular spelling or to a list of words provided by the teacher. It can be played in a small or large group or as a whole class.

ACTIVITY 7

Spelling Snap

Small group game for 2 to 5 players.

Sight words from NLS word lists made into laminated 'playing cards' and put into mixed sets, with words from all years up to class's current year in sets of 20 or a multiple of the group size closest to 20.

Pupils deal 2 matching sets of shuffled cards, face down.

Play normal 'snap' game except that all group shout each word as it is turned over.

Pupils win any matched pairs they 'snapped'. The player with the most pairs wins.

ACTIVITY 8

Spelling Match

3 to 5 players

Two sets of the above playing cards, shuffled into one big set and spread on table top, face down.

Each player turns 2 cards in sequence and all say each word.

Every player tries to remember where the matching words are.

They win by matching pairs. The player with the most matched pairs wins.

Examples of Other Activities:

Speaking the 'writing voice'	"Who can make me up a sentence beginning with..." "Who can make up a sentence with the word XXX in?"
Correcting grammar	"This is what Marmaduke just said to me – what's wrong with it?" "Here's a piece of writing Marmaduke gave me – what's wrong with it?" 'Talking posh' and having 'posh' lessons.
Correcting Marmaduke's writing	Whole class edit 'Marmaduke's writing' on OHP or white board. In two's – edit on hard copy.
Opener and Connective Fans	"How many connectives could join these two sentences?" "How does the meaning change if you use this connective or that one?" "Which of these connectives would make a good opener for this sentence?"
Up-levelling	"Tell your friend which two words you would change and into what, to up-level this sentence." "Insert two 'WOW' words into this sentence." "Change the structure of this sentence to up-level it." "Change the opening of this sentence to up-level it." Give pupils three or more simple sentences to up-level together. Give pupils Marmaduke's writing to up-level for him – whole class or in pairs.
Punctuation Games	"Shout on 3 – what would come at the end of this sentence?" "Draw on your white boards – what would..." "Draw in the air – what would..." "Shout and draw in the air – what would..." "Draw a piece of punctuation on your friend's back with your finger, s/he must guess what it was and make up a sentence using it" Kung Fu punctuation Give pupils Marmaduke's writing with the punctuation missing – whole class or in 2s correct it for him. Practise and then read out sentences and paragraphs with the punctuation omitted, pupils name punctuation at the right points as they read.

The following were prepared by Michelle Wraith, Big Writing and Literacy consultant:

VCOP challenges

1. You have 60 seconds, write as many openers ending in '– ly' as you can think of.
- Share your words with a friend
- Write as many sentences as you can using your words as openers, you have 5 minutes to do this task
- Share your sentences with a friend
- 'Up-level' at least 2 of your sentences

2. You have 60 seconds, write as many openers ending in '– ing' as you can think of.
- Share your words with a friend
- Write as many sentences as you can using your words as openers, you have 5 minutes to do this task
- Share your sentences with a friend
- 'Up-level' at least 2 of your sentences

3. You have 60 seconds, how many connectives which would be good as openers can you think of?
- Share your words with a friend
- Write as many sentences as you can using your words as openers, you have 5 minutes to do this task
- Share your sentences with a friend
- 'Up-level' at least 2 of your sentences

Openers from sequence words

Write some interesting sentences that open with these time connectives.
Make sure you use your VC and P.

First –

Then –

Next –

After –

Soon –

After a while –

Before –

Meanwhile –

When –

Later –

Shortly before –

Shortly after –

Finally –

Eventually –

Goal scorers of the week

Why do I like these sentences? Think about the VCOP
that has been used. Underline (or highlight) the part
that you think 'up-levelled' the sentence.

- The light dimmed. I took a glance at the beast whilst
  I still had time.

- It was a gigantic, green monster. It was a... a... cyclop!

- Although I might have killed it, I was still petrified!

- My heart was pounding, pounding so fast I couldn't
  breathe.

- How was I going to escape? Would the beast try to
  eat me?

- Hopefully someone would hear but unfortunately no-
  one came.

- How was I going to escape? Would the beast eat me?

- The big, sharp teeth, the horrid roar, the green and
  black scales, they made me tremble.

- It opened its mouth and let out a stomach turning,
  monstrous and terrifying roar.

- It had transformed into a giant, drooling dragon.

- The monster, or whatever it was, was too horrible to
  describe. It was vile!

Missing punctuation

**Correct the following sentences, think about the use of
capital letters and punctuation.**

Why was she looking at me

Whilst he was concerned for his own safety he knew he
must go On

violently the enemy thrust himself against the wall of
Soldiers

Throughout the evening the atmosphere became tense
Why was everyone so nervous

Help me now He screamed

despite his fear of the darkness he stumbled through to the heart of the forest

finally he was free He couldnt believe his luck

Please clare please let me join your gang lucy pleaded

Can i have the key to the dungeon asked the prison officer

yesterday Class 6 visited the ancient ruin in the grounds of the Abbey

Initially you will need Paper scissors glue paint and brushes

Rosie who was a greedy girl ate several cakes daily when she returned from School

How many of you have pets at Home inquired the teacher

After months of careful work the scientists finally opened the tomb It was empty

Entering the crowded room he couldnt believe his eyes It was a _____ (also complete the sentence).

The number of different languages currently about 6000 is decreasing rapidly

fionas family were extremely rich

why is it so hard to know which type of punctuation to use she asked the teacher

- Which of the words on the wall could you use in:

- a report
- an explanation
- a story
- a set of instructions
- a letter to a friend
- a television advert
- a recount

Ambitious vocabulary

Look at the 'wow words' on your class display.

- Do you know the meaning of all the words? Talk to your partner. Use a dictionary if necessary.

- Think of an interesting sentence that contains one, two or even three of these words. Tell your partner.

- Choose your favourite 6 words from the display. Write a sentence for each word (remember VCOP).

- Try to describe the word to your partner without actually saying the word.

- Spell the word letter by letter to your partner. Can they say what the word is without writing it down?

- Which of the words are adverbs? Are there any adjectives?

Warm up activity

Sort the following words into the chart below.

funny	green	supportive
kind	dominating	sensitive
generous	strict	enthusiastic
playful	fearsome	jolly
warm	ferocious	stern
boring	stubborn	unsupportive
efficient	cold	grumpy
friendly	bossy	organised
organised	uncaring	aggressive
unkind	chatty	caring
dedicated	passionate	furry
lethargic	fantastic	impatient
inspirational	intellectually challenged	approachable

You can make up your own heading for the fourth column. You may want to use some of the words in all of the columns.

Teacher	Monster	Friend	

Can you think of any other ambitious words to describe the headings in the chart above?

APPENDIX 3
'ALL WRITE NOW' MATERIALS

With thanks to Ian McCollum.

All Write Now! from ROWA!	
Adjectives [Ambitious Words] **Card 1**	
I was chased by five _____ dogs. [panic]	
a	upset
b	vicious
c	angry

All Write Now! from ROWA!	
Adjectives [Ambitious Words] **Card 2**	
The _____ woods frightened the rider's horse. [spooky]	
a	extraordinary
b	dark
c	menacing

All Write Now! from ROWA!	
Adjectives [Ambitious Words] **Card 3**	
John was lost in a _____ fog. [sinister]	
a	dense
b	grey
c	bright

All Write Now! from ROWA!	
Adjectives [Ambitious Words] **Card 4**	
The _____ driver was going much too fast. [danger]	
a	awful
b	sensible
c	crazy

All Write Now! from ROWA!	
Adjectives [Ambitious Words] **Card 5**	
The _____ fire destroyed the factory. [serious]	
a	roaring
b	disastrous
c	timid

All Write Now! from ROWA!	
Adjectives [Ambitious Words] **Card 6**	
A _____ pack of wolves stalked the flock of sheep. [crafty]	
a	cunning
b	bad
c	delightful

All Write Now! from ROWA!	
Adjectives [Ambitious Words] **Card 7**	
The _____ elephant tore down the tree. [biggest]	
a	microscopic
b	bulky
c	enormous

All Write Now! from ROWA!	
Adjectives [Ambitious Words] **Card 8**	
The _____ car was towed away. [after a crash]	
a	shattered
b	cheerful
c	wrecked

All Write Now! from ROWA!	
Adverbs [Ambitious Words] **Card 1**	
The tiger _____ stalked her prey. [sinister]	
a	carelessly
b	silently
c	slowly

All Write Now! from ROWA!	
Adverbs [Ambitious Words] **Card 2**	
The men dug _____ to save the trapped child. [urgent]	
a	easily
b	quickly
c	frantically

All Write Now! from ROWA!	
Adverbs [Ambitious Words] **Card 3**	
He handled the gun _____ and it went off. [stupid]	
a	recklessly
b	carefully
c	delicately

All Write Now! from ROWA!	
Adverbs [Ambitious Words] **Card 4**	
Two boys were fighting _____ in the yard. [nasty]	
a	horribly
b	pleasantly
c	viciously

All Write Now! from ROWA!	
Adverbs [Ambitious Words] **Card 5**	
I walked _____ down the stairs. [nervous]	
a	timidly
b	slowly
c	viciously

All Write Now! from ROWA!	
Adverbs [Ambitious Words] **Card 6**	
The bully spoke _____ to the little boy. [horrible]	
a	unkindly
b	kindly
c	aggressively

All Write Now! from ROWA!	
Adverbs [Ambitious Words] **Card 7**	
The policewoman followed _____ after the suspect. [in secret]	
a	cautiously
b	stealthily
c	noisily

All Write Now! from ROWA!	
Adverbs [Ambitious Words] **Card 8**	
The fire roared _____ through the town. [damage]	
a	rapidly
b	extremely
c	destructively

All Write Now! from ROWA!	
Adverbs [Ambitious Words] **Card 9**	
The detectives _____ investigated the robbery. [professional]	
a	painstakingly
b	accidentally
c	slowly

All Write Now! from ROWA!	
Adverbs [Ambitious Words] **Card 10**	
The girls climbed _____ up the tree to escape from the dog. [panic]	
a	lazily
b	steadily
c	swiftly

All Write Now! from ROWA!	
Adverbs [Ambitious Words] **Card 11**	
The soldiers fought _____ despite the odds. [brave]	
a	fearlessly
b	nervously
c	well

All Write Now! from ROWA!	
Adverbs [Ambitious Words] **Card 12**	
The sun shone _____ on the garden. [too hot]	
a	remotely
b	intensely
c	brightly

All Write Now! from ROWA!	
Adverbs [Ambitious Words] **Card 13**	
We walked _____ away from the bullies. [very fast]	
a	quickly
b	casually
c	hastily

All Write Now! from ROWA!	
Adverbs [Ambitious Words] **Card 14**	
The sky-diver drifted _____ to earth after her parachute opened. [calm]	
a	delicately
b	heavily
c	silently

All Write Now! from ROWA!	
Adverbs [Ambitious Words] **Card 15**	
The racehorse galloped _____ to the front. [easy winner]	
a	exhaustedly
b	effortlessly
c	rapidly

All Write Now! from ROWA!	
Adverbs [Ambitious Words] **Card 16**	
The old door swung _____ open. [spooky]	
a	quietly
b	sweetly
c	noiselessly

All Write Now! from ROWA!	
Apostrophe **Card 1**	
The boy's ran down the street.	
a	Apostrophe correct
b	No apostrophe needed
c	Apostrophe in wrong place

All Write Now! from ROWA!	
Apostrophe **Card 2**	
There are 2 wheels' on my bike.	
a	Apostrophe correct
b	No apostrophe needed
c	Apostrophe in wrong place

All Write Now! from ROWA!	
Apostrophe **Card 3**	
My uncle's hat blew away.	
a	Apostrophe correct
b	No apostrophe needed
c	Apostrophe in wrong place

All Write Now! from ROWA!	
Apostrophe **Card 4**	
You're my best mate.	
a	Apostrophe correct
b	No apostrophe needed
c	Apostrophe in wrong place

All Write Now! from ROWA!	
Apostrophe **Card 5**	
I ca'nt swim very fast.	
a	Apostrophe correct
b	No apostrophe needed
c	Apostrophe in wrong place

All Write Now! from ROWA!	
Apostrophe **Card 6**	
Four girls' went for a walk.	
a	Apostrophe correct
b	No apostrophe needed
c	Apostrophe in wrong place

All Write Now! from ROWA!	
Apostrophe **Card 7**	
Jakes' house is down that road.	
a	Apostrophe correct
b	No apostrophe needed
c	Apostrophe in wrong place

All Write Now! from ROWA!	
Apostrophe **Card 8**	
Seven boy's boots went missing.	
a	Apostrophe correct
b	No apostrophe needed
c	Apostrophe in wrong place

All Write Now! Boardgame Answers

APOSTROPHES			
	'Best answer'	**'OK answer'**	**Definitely no good**
Card 1	No apostrophe needed		Apostrophe correct Apostrophe wrong place
Card 2	No apostrophe needed		Apostrophe correct Apostrophe wrong place
Card 3	Apostrophe correct		No apostrophe needed Apostrophe wrong place
Card 4	Apostrophe correct		No apostrophe needed Apostrophe wrong place
Card 5	Apostrophe wrong place		No apostrophe needed Apostrophe correct
Card 6	No apostrophe needed		Apostrophe correct Apostrophe wrong place
Card 7	Apostrophe wrong place		No apostrophe needed Apostrophe correct
Card 8	Apostrophe wrong place		No apostrophe needed Apostrophe correct
Card 9	Apostrophe correct		No apostrophe needed Apostrophe wrong place
Card 10	Apostrophe correct		No apostrophe needed Apostrophe wrong place
Card 11	No apostrophe needed		Apostrophe correct Apostrophe wrong place
Card 12	Apostrophe wrong place		No apostrophe needed Apostrophe correct
Card 13	Apostrophe correct		No apostrophe needed Apostrophe wrong place
Card 14	No apostrophe needed		Apostrophe correct Apostrophe wrong place
Card 15	Apostrophe correct		No apostrophe needed Apostrophe wrong place
Card 16	Apostrophe wrong place		No apostrophe needed Apostrophe correct

APPENDIX 3

'ALL WRITE NOW' MATERIALS

	'Best answer'	'OK answer'	Definitely no good
SPEECH MARKS			
Card 1	No Speech Marks needed		Speech Marks correct One set in right place
Card 2	One set in right place		Speech Marks correct No Speech Marks needed
Card 3	Speech Marks correct		One set in right place No Speech Marks needed
Card 4	One set in right place		Speech Marks correct No Speech Marks needed
Card 5	No Speech Marks needed		Speech Marks correct One set in right place
Card 6	Speech Marks correct		One set in right place No Speech Marks needed
Card 7	One set in right place		Speech Marks correct No Speech Marks needed
Card 8	One set in right place		Speech Marks correct No Speech Marks needed
Card 9	One set in right place		Speech Marks correct No Speech Marks needed
Card 10	No Speech Marks needed		Speech Marks correct One set in right place
Card 11	No Speech Marks needed		Speech Marks correct One set in right place
Card 12	Speech Marks correct		One set in right place No Speech Marks needed
Card 13	One set in right place		Speech Marks correct No Speech Marks needed
Card 14	No Speech Marks needed		Speech Marks correct One set in right place
Card 15	One set in right place		Speech Marks correct No Speech Marks needed
Card 16	Speech Marks correct		One set in right place No Speech Marks needed

	'Best answer'	'OK answer'	Definitely no good
OPENERS			
Card 1	If		Soon & Next
Card 2	After a while	Last time	Another day
Card 3	Despite		Due to & Soon
Card 4	Soon		Having decided & Although
Card 5	Although		Having decided & Because
Card 6	Before	When & After	
Card 7	Immediately		Last time & When
Card 8	Afterwards		Another thing & Because
Card 9	Another thing		Although & Also
Card 10	First	During the night	Before
Card 11	Shouting boys		Last time & Although I
Card 12	Sometimes	First	Because
Card 13	Twice	Fortunately	Because
Card 14	Also		Eventually & Tomorrow
Card 15	Nervously		If & After
Card 16	Eventually	Another thing	When

CONNECTIVES

	'Best answer'	'OK answer'	Definitely no good
Card 1	although		after & because
Card 2	and	when	if
Card 3	as & when	also	
Card 4	but		despite & when
Card 5	but	as well as & because	
Card 6	because	in addition	so
Card 7	but	however	then
Card 8	then		because & during
Card 9	because		but & also
Card 10	and		because & despite
Card 11	but		although & while
Card 12	however	in addition	although
Card 13	but		then & before
Card 14	even though	and	because
Card 15	then		when & as soon as
Card 16	and & but		because

VERBS [Ambitious Words]

	'Best answer'	'OK answer'	Definitely no good
Card 1	charged	strolled	talked
Card 2	hurtled	ran	wandered
Card 3	tore & hacked		washed
Card 4	drifted	climbed	leapt
Card 5	roared	flew	drifted
Card 6	smashed & drilled		passed
Card 7	rescued	helped	dived
Card 8	yelled	moaned	sang
Card 9	swerved & skidded	was	
Card 10	vaulted		helped & fell
Card 11	plummeted	fell	ascended
Card 12	toppled	broke	healed
Card 13	fought	sailed	collided
Card 14	shattered & rocked		built
Card 15	leapt	climbed	strolled
Card 16	erupted	came	emerged

ADJECTIVES [Ambitious Words]

	'Best answer'	'OK answer'	Definitely no good
Card 1	vicious	angry	upset
Card 2	menacing	dark & extraordinary	
Card 3	dense	grey	bright
Card 4	crazy	awful	sensible
Card 5	disastrous & roaring		timid
Card 6	cunning	bad	delightful
Card 7	enormous	bulky	microscopic
Card 8	shattered & wrecked		cheerful
Card 9	ancient	dusty	reading
Card 10	exceptional	good	appalling
Card 11	microscopic & minute		massive
Card 12	blustery		hurricane & solid
Card 13	monstrous	large	charming
Card 14	towering		insignificant & wooden
Card 15	awesome		awful & average
Card 16	shadowy & gloomy		attractive

ADVERBS [Ambitious Words]		
	'Best answer'	'OK answer'	Definitely no good

	'Best answer'	'OK answer'	Definitely no good
Card 1	silently	slowly	carelessly
Card 2	frantically	quickly	easily
Card 3	recklessly		carefully & delicately
Card 4	viciously	horribly	pleasantly
Card 5	timidly	slowly	aggressively
Card 6	aggressively	unkindly	kindly
Card 7	cautiously & stealthily		noisily
Card 8	destructively	rapidly	extremely
Card 9	painstakingly		accidentally & slowly
Card 10	swiftly		lazily & steadily
Card 11	fearlessly	well	nervously
Card 12	intensely	brightly	remotely
Card 13	hastily	quickly	casually
Card 14	delicately	silently	heavily
Card 15	effortlessly	rapidly	exhaustedly
Card 16	noiselessly	quietly	sweetly

All Write Now! from ROWA!

Connectives **Card 1**

You're my best mate. You never call me. (unhappy)

a	after
b	although
c	because

All Write Now! from ROWA!

Connectives **Card 2**

My sister dropped her bag. A boy ran off with it. (shock/horror)

a	and
b	if
c	when

All Write Now! from ROWA!

Connectives **Card 3**

The cat sat at the top of a tree. The dog barked loudly. (scared)

a	when
b	as
c	also

All Write Now! from ROWA!

Connectives **Card 4**

It's my birthday. I've only had two cards. (surprise)

a	despite
b	but
c	when

All Write Now! from ROWA!

Connectives **Card 5**

The door is locked. The key is missing. (panic)

a	as well as
b	but
c	because

All Write Now! from ROWA!

Connectives **Card 6**

I'm late for school. The bus was late. (excuse)

a	in addition
b	so
c	because

All Write Now! from ROWA!

Connectives **Card 7**

The test starts at 10:15. Be ready by the door at 10:00. (just in case)

a	however
b	then
c	but

All Write Now! from ROWA!

Connectives **Card 8**

The church clock struck 12. The doors slowly opened. (suspense)

a	because
b	during
c	then

All Write Now! from ROWA!

Connectives **Card 9**

You wait in here. I will fetch the others. (instruction)

a	because
b	but
c	also

All Write Now! from ROWA!	
Connectives **Card 10**	
There are three tables in here. There are three more in the next room.(need)	
a	and
b	because
c	despite

All Write Now! from ROWA!	
Connectives **Card 11**	
The laces in my trainers have broken. I brought some new ones. (relief)	
a	while
b	although
c	in addition

All Write Now! from ROWA!	
Connectives **Card 12**	
My Dad's car would not start. It had run out of petrol. (reason why)	
a	however
b	although
c	in addition

All Write Now! from ROWA!	
Connectives **Card 13**	
Ian needed new football boots. He had no money. (problem)	
a	then
b	but
c	before

All Write Now! from ROWA!	
Connectives **Card 14**	
The house was very cold. All the windows were closed. (reason)	
a	and
b	because
c	even though

All Write Now! from ROWA!	
Connectives **Card 15**	
The train stopped. The passengers got down onto the platform. (next)	
a	when
b	then
c	as soon as

All Write Now! from ROWA!	
Connectives **Card 16**	
Four people got into the lift. Four people used the stairs. (no room)	
a	and
b	but
c	because

'Find a Word'

This is an occasional activity for groups of children who need to practise writing instructions. Also useful for Team Building and delegation skills.

Team A [the 'Hide Team'] selects a word of a previously agreed number of letters. The word is typed onto a computer and printed onto a label. The label is then cut into vertical strips with one letter on each strip. The A writes a clue to help Team C to recreate the finished word.

The strips are hidden around a specified area and Team B is given an opportunity to locate the strips without removing them. Team B then has responsibility to write directions/instructions to enable Team C to find the strips more quickly. Team C then uses the instructions to find the strips and then uses the clue provided by Team A to reassemble the word.Ω

If you wish to score the event to make it competitive, all 3 stages should be timed or time limited.

To be agreed beforehand

- Number of letters in word
- Size and colour of font
- Size and colour of label
- Specified area for hiding [e.g. own classroom/corridors/playground in summer etc.]

'Rules'
Letters should always be in plain view [can be seen without having to move anything]. Letters should never be indangerous places. Letters should never be in limited access areas.

E.g.
above head height
close to doors
close to radiators [in winter]

✍ All Write Now!

Make up a story

Character	Place	Object
Spider-man	A beach on a hot day	A raw carrot
Winnie the Pooh	Under the sea	A bicycle pump
Robin Hood	In an enormous cave	A sack of potatoes
Little Red Riding Hood	On a drifting iceberg	An empty pop can
The Prime Minister	Locked in a cellar	A remote control car
The Queen	A skyscraper roof	A bucket with a hole
Our Headteacher	In a hot air balloon	A broken computer
A tall policeman	Inside a dustbin	An electric drill
A happy doctor	In a dark forest	A bent spoon
A circus clown	On the moon	A baby elephant
A young musician	In a dentist's surgery	A pair of scissors
You	On a sinking ship	A paper aeroplane

Suggestion:	Print this page on 3 different coloured cards. Cut each page into 3 vertical strips and then mix up the colours to make 3 separate game sets. Cut horizontally to make 3 sets of 12 cards for each game pack.

Game 1: Student draws one card from each pack and then has [?] seconds to make up an explanation why that character ended up in that place, with that object.

Game 2: Student draws one card from each pack and writes a short story which features at some stage, the character, the place and the object.

Game 3: As in game one or two, but featuring 2 or more characters and two or more objects in one place.

All Write Now! from ROWA!	
Openers **Card 1**	
...you come over here I will help you.	
a	If
b	Soon
c	Next

All Write Now! from ROWA!	
Openers **Card 2**	
...I began to think I had gone the wrong way.	
a	Another day
b	Last time
c	After a while

All Write Now! from ROWA!	
Openers **Card 3**	
...Tom's hard work, he didn't get a good score in the test.	
a	Due to
b	Despite
c	Soon

All Write Now! from ROWA!	
Openers **Card 4**	
... it will be time to got to bed.	
a	Soon
b	Although
c	Having decided

All Write Now! from ROWA!	
Openers **Card 5**	
...you are taller than me, I can run faster than you!	
a	Having decided
b	Although
c	Because

All Write Now! from ROWA!	
Openers **Card 6**	
...the bridge fell there was a terrible storm	
a	When
b	After
c	Before

All Write Now! from ROWA!	
Openers **Card 7**	
... the enormous spider began to eat his prey.	
a	When
b	Immediately
c	Last time

All Write Now! from ROWA!	
Openers **Card 8**	
... I ran home very quickly.	
a	Afterwards
b	Another thing
c	Because

All Write Now! from ROWA!	
Openers **Card 9**	
... we like to eat is curry.	
a	Also
b	Although
c	Another thing

All Write Now! from ROWA!	
Openers **Card 10**	
... I want you pick up that paper.	
a	First
b	Before
c	During the night

All Write Now! from ROWA!	
Openers **Card 11**	
... ran down the street.	
a	Although
b	Last time
c	Shouting boys

All Write Now! from ROWA!	
Openers **Card 12**	
... my friends come to my house for tea.	
a	Because
b	Sometimes
c	First

All Write Now! from ROWA!	
Openers **Card 13**	
... the little boy wandered across the road.	
a	Because
b	Fortunately
c	Twice

All Write Now! from ROWA!	
Openers **Card 14**	
... it's time you tried harder with your Maths.	
a	Also
b	Eventually
c	Tomorrow

All Write Now! from ROWA!	
Openers **Card 15**	
... I went up the stairs.	
a	Nervously
b	If
c	After

All Write Now! from ROWA!	
Openers **Card 16**	
... the boys agreed to stop fighting.	
a	Eventually
b	Another thing
c	When

All Write Now! from ROWA!	
Speech Marks **Card 1**	
"The man told me to" go over there.	
a	Speech marks correct
b	One set in right place
c	No speech marks needed

All Write Now! from ROWA!	
Speech Marks **Card 2**	
"My name is Tracey, she said"	
a	Speech marks correct
b	One set in right place
c	No speech marks needed

All Write Now! from ROWA!

Speech Marks **Card 3**

"What does that cost?" she asked.

a	Speech marks correct
b	One set in right place
c	No speech marks needed

All Write Now! from ROWA!

Speech Marks **Card 4**

"You're my best mate, said Pete."

a	Speech marks correct
b	One set in right place
c	No speech marks needed

All Write Now! from ROWA!

Speech Marks **Card 5**

Tom asked "the way to town."

a	Speech marks correct
b	One set in right place
c	No speech marks needed

All Write Now! from ROWA!

Speech Marks **Card 6**

"Help, I'm stuck!" shouted the man.

a	Speech marks correct
b	One set in right place
c	No speech marks needed

All Write Now! from ROWA!

Speech Marks **Card 7**

Who is he?" asked the boy"

a	Speech marks correct
b	One set in right place
c	No speech marks needed

All Write Now! from ROWA!

Speech Marks **Card 8**

"Where is" John? asked Adam.

a	Speech marks correct
b	One set in right place
c	No speech marks needed

All Write Now! from ROWA!

Speech Marks **Card 9**

"Stop" thief, shouted the policeman.

a	Speech marks correct
b	One set in right place
c	No speech marks needed

All Write Now! from ROWA!

Speech Marks **Card 10**

My mum asked me, "where I had been."

a	Speech marks correct
b	One set in right place
c	No speech marks needed

All Write Now! from ROWA!

Speech Marks **Card 11**

I asked the new boy "what his name was".

a	Speech marks correct
b	One set in right place
c	No speech marks needed

All Write Now! from ROWA!

Speech Marks **Card 12**

"Tom is here!" everyone shouted.

a	Speech marks correct
b	One set in right place
c	No speech marks needed

All Write Now! from ROWA!

Speech Marks **Card 13**

"I said, the shop is over there."

a	Speech marks correct
b	One set in right place
c	No speech marks needed

All Write Now! from ROWA!

Speech Marks **Card 14**

"She asked me what my name was."

a	Speech marks correct
b	One set in right place
c	No speech marks needed

All Write Now! from ROWA!

Speech Marks **Card 15**

Leave me alone!" shouted the child".

a	Speech marks correct
b	One set in right place
c	No speech marks needed

All Write Now! from ROWA!

Speech Marks **Card 16**

"I want to come!" said the boy.

a	Speech marks correct
b	One set in right place
c	No speech marks needed

IF YOU HAVE FOUND THIS TASTER OF THE EXCELLENT WORK OF THE 'ALL WRITE NOW' TEAM CONTACT THE READ ON WRITE AWAY PROJECT, DERBYSHIRE, IN ORDER TO PURCHASE THE FULL CD ROM.

APPENDIX 4
'WRITE ON TRACK'

An intervention to raise standards from Level 2 to Level 3 at Key Stage 2.

The following intervention has been planned to support pupils in Key Stage 2 still working at Level 2. It is intended to take place by TEMPORARY withdrawal for a period of up to eight weeks.

It should be taught by an experienced and well respected teacher or Senior Manager.

It should be explained to the pupils as recognition that the education system has let them down. They possibly believe they are 'no good' at writing, and that this is not true. They have been specially chosen to be given special teaching because the school knows how to help them to be the Level 4/5 writers they truly should be.

This intervention is planned to take up to 8 weeks. It is planned to be delivered to either 1) a withdrawal group of up to 20 pupils OR 2) a low achieving set in a large school.

 NB We do not advocate setting for Literacy as it removes the best role models and opportunities for good peer support.

The series of lessons should be taught by a lively and exciting teacher, who may be a Senior Manager. It is important that he/she has the respect of the children. The class teacher and teacher teaching the target group should be discussing outcomes and adjusting the next week's planning together.

Pupils in Lower Key Stage 2 assessed at Level 2 should have one one-hour lesson a day for four days a week for up to eight weeks. This should replace the standard literacy hour, and thus is most suitable for pupils in Years 3 and 4, to allow time in Upper Key Stage 2 to 'catch up' on the text types pupils will miss through this intervention. In addition, they should have the weekly 'Big Writing' on the fifth day, which may be either Thursday or Friday.

The lesson should be in a pleasant but private environment (to protect self-esteem) and will require at minimum:
- a whiteboard
- flip chart and felt tips
- an overhead projector
- laminated A4 story structure cards for each pupil
- laminated playing cards for the word lists
- opener and connective fans
- VCOP display the same as in the classroom
- Story structure display the same as in the classroom

The teacher MUST lead at a brisk and lively pace, and encourage pupils to work at the same pace, using constant praise for quick responses.

 NB Each 15 minute 'Step' is always sub-divided yet again, often into oral and written or group response / pupil discussion. This is to reflect concentration times, which are generally the number of years a pupil has been alive plus one. A nine year old child can usually only concentrate for 10 minutes before taking a 'brain break'. Teaching should reflect this by 'chunking' input and activity into blocks of ten minutes or less before changing to the other.

The module MUST be adapted weekly in response to pupils' learning and attitudes and the focus of the weekly 'Big Writing' lesson, however the first week may be delivered as a standard week. Only week 1 has been provided as a similar range of activities are delivered each week.

WEEK 1

The teacher introduces the module to the pupils. Use the term 'module' to give the intervention status. The following explanation is crucial for pupils' motivation, self-esteem and self-belief. It should be delivered confidently and sincerely, and pupils should be involved in a discussion about how they feel about themselves as writers.

Explain to pupils that the education system has failed them. Acknowledge that you know they feel they are not good writers, and that they do not do as well as some of their friends at writing. Tell them that this is not their fault, and that you KNOW they can be as good as everyone else at writing, and that taking part in this module will enable this. Explain that children start school in England before the age that most of them are ready to learn, and that many children in every single school across the country have gaps in their basic skills that prevent them from achieving their very best at writing. Tell them that this module will close the gaps.

Use constant praise and instant rewards throughout the module. Chocolate footballs are highly successful motivators, and should be accompanied by the phrase, 'Well done, you have scored a goal'. Negotiation may be needed with parents, to gain permission for short term use of none-healthy motivators in order to re-affect the disaffected, however, if this is not achievable, grapes, award charts with footballs that move along the goal scores or football stickers could be considered.

NB After the eight weeks the use of chocolate as a motivator may be abandoned as visible success now takes over as the prime motivator.

DAY 1

 NB A summary overview of this intervention is provided on the facing pages.

The teacher model-writes on whiteboard, leading the composition, but with pupils calling out the spelling and punctuation in unison.

 NB If pupils do not identify the need for something, e.g. full stops and capital letters, the teacher should not record them. If no pupil then recognises the need, the teacher leads the pupils in reading back the writing and asks if anyone can spot what is wrong. If no-one can she/he then explains the need for sentence punctuation, reading the writing herself/himself to show how the reader naturally pauses for the end of a sentence, and saying the writer needs to help the reader by showing where one sentence ends by use of a full stop, and where a new sentence begins by use of a capital letter.

From this point, praise highly when pupils call out, 'Full stop, capital letter' in the shared writing.

The writing is ALWAYS to the same model and must be written at Level 1 (no connectives or complex sentences). However, it must be written neatly in the school's joined handwriting style.

Step 1 (15 minutes)
The teacher calls each word in turn, and records it AS the group call out the spelling. Each of the four days it begins as follows:

Today is _____(1)
It is a _____(2) day

(1) = *name of the day, e.g. Monday.*
(2) = *type of weather, e.g. 'sunny', 'windy', 'cloudy', 'rainy'.*

The teacher then leads one further sentence relevant to the pupils, of the type we would call 'news', e.g:

'We are working hard at our writing'.
OR 'We are going to be excellent writers by
_____'. (End of the term)
OR 'Mr. X talked to us in assembly today'.
OR 'The school team is playing a match today'.
OR 'Liam brought his spider to school today'.

The writing must not be more than 3 sentences as the copying must not become a chore. When it is completed on the board, the whole group read it back together and discuss any spellings that gave difficulty, or the sentence punctuation if that gave difficulty. (10 minutes maximum)

Handwriting focus:
The group re-read the writing and are then asked to copy it in their 'best' cursive writing. A very special writing book or file should have been provided for this module, one not normally used in the school and bought especially to motivate the pupils. Also, pupils should have special roller ball pens only used for this lesson.

Praise for improving handwriting as they copy. (5 minutes)

Step 2 (15 minutes)
Children work with teacher to add a list of at least 3 sentences to the model writing, using the same technique. Because these pupils are KS2, this does not have to be the Level 1 type of list referred to in previous publications, i.e. all opening structures do not have to be alike, (e.g. 'I like........, I like.........., I like..........'.) However, it must still be written at Level 1, i.e. in simple sentences with no detail. Whenever possible, the list should be relevant to the group, and/or reflect their interests.

 Examples:

1.   Our school is big.
         It has a playing field.
         There are two hundred children in our school.

2.   We learn to play soccer at school.
         The school team is good.
         Some of us support _____. (Local team e.g. Leeds United)

3.   We live in _____. (Name of city, town, village or district)
         It has a _____. (Name of key feature).
         We are all proud to live here.

Spelling focus:
The group reads the list through, discusses any spellings that gave difficulty and calls out some other words with the same spelling, which the TEACHER records on the flip chart or at one end of the board. (10 minutes)

They then read it again before copying it neatly as a continuation of their earlier writing. (5 minutes)

Step 3 (15 minutes)

 NB nothing is to be written down by the pupils. The model for this should be a Level 4/5 model.

VCOP activities, ('stocking fillers' as described in 'Strategies for Immediate Impact on Writing'). Should be the SAME examples as the teacher used in 'Big Writing' the previous week.

May include any of the following types of activities over the weeks of the intervention:

1. Up-levelling 3 Level 1 sentences on the flip chart (NOT the ones from the writing).

2. Using flash cards with ambitious vocabulary on, 'Who can make me up a sentence with _____ in?' (Name the word). If pupils are new to the words, let them work in 2s and feed back.

3. Using flash cards with openers and connectives on, 'Who can make me up a sentence beginning with_____?' (Name the word). If pupils are new to the words, let them work in 2s and feed back.

4. Using opener and connective fans (as described in 'Strategies for Immediate Impact on Writing Standards, 2003).

5. Using individual whiteboards to record an opener or a connective they might use between 2 simple sentences the teacher gives orally.

6. Drawing (in the air) and say/shout piece of punctuation you might find on the end of this sentence... (all oral). The teacher makes up sentences and says them, e.g: 'Go out!' 'Is it raining?' 'All of a sudden.....' (See also 'Kung Fu Punctuation', Appendix 2).

7. Playing punctuation pyramid games. (p162 Strategies for Immediate Impact on Writing Standards 2003)

8. Playing Opener and Connective games. (See 'Activities' Appendix 2)

9. Giving a processed paragraph with no punctuation (from the imaginary friend?). In 2s practise reading it, inserting orally the punctuation required to provide the pauses and intonation implied, and drawing in the air as they say it. Then re-read as a group, all naming and drawing the punctuation as they proceed.

10. Example: The young boy crept into the gloomy house he paused by a partially open door with a trembling hand he pushed it further open it creaked loudly on rusted hinges all of a sudden something flew at him aaargh he screamed as he turned and ran

 NB nothing is to be written down by the children. The model for this should be a Level 4 /5 model. The Senior Manager should support in the development of further examples. This is an ideal context for applying Kung Fu Punctuation, see Appendix 1.

The paragraph might be read back as follows;

The young boy crept into the gloomy house FULLSTOP (DRAW AS SAY). CAPITAL H (DRAW AS SAY) He paused by a partially open door FULL STOP (DRAW AS SAY). CAPITAL W (DRAW AS SAY) With a trembling hand he pushed it further open FU LLSTOP (DRAW AS SAY). CAPITAL I (DRAW AS SAY) It creaked loudly on rusted hinges FULLSTOP (DRAW AS SAY). CAPITAL A (DRAW AS SAY) All of a sudden something flew at him FULLSTOP or EXCLAMATION MARK or ELLIPSES (DRAW AS SAY) SPEECH MARKS/CAPITAL A (DRAW AS SAY), "Aaaargh EXCLAMATION MARK / SPEECH MARKS (DRAW AS SAY)!" he screamed as he turned and ran ELLIPSES OR FULL STOP (DRAW AS SAY)...

Step 4 (15 minutes)

Sight word activities:
Start with Reception word list from NLS and work through to Year 2 over the weeks. Include the key words from the week's writing, so for this first week the words, 'Today', 'is', 'we', 'are', 'going', 'to'. Begin with 10 words per week as all children will probably know some; adjust up and down according to performance.

Make sets of laminated flashcards of keywords to use in any one of the following ways:

1. Hold up flash cards, pupils call out and spell

2. Give 2 shuffled sets between two pupils, play 'Snap' to win the pairs, saying each word out loud as it is turned over. When a child wins a pair, he/she must say and say and spell the word.

3. Give 2 sets between 3 or 4 pupils, shuffle and spread out face down, play turning and matching to win the pairs, saying each word out loud as it is turned over. When a child wins a pair, he/she must say and say and spell the word.

Note carefully/record any words pupils are hesitant on spelling. (10 minutes)
Briskly re-read model writing off whiteboard, recap any VCOP that have caused difficulties and re-read any up-levelling or punctuation paragraphs completed. Praise and reward. Close lesson. (5 minutes)

1 OVERVIEW

STEP 1 Total = 15 mins 10 mins 5 mins	Teacher calls each word in turn. Pupils spell and say punctuation First 2 lines ALWAYS same structure Third line is created by class Teacher scribes on board in school style. All read back together. Each pupil copies 3 lines in 'best' school style.	1. Today is Monday. (Day of week) 2. It is a sunny day. (Type of weather) 3. e.g. We are all very good writers
STEP 2 Total = 15 mins 10 mins 5 mins	Group work together to add 3 more simple sentences. Pupils call out spelling for words as teacher scribes. Any spellings that give difficulty are underlined, then recorded as a separate list on flip chart, spelling out loud as go. If time, pupils call out other words with same root. The group then reads the three sentences together. Each pupil copies the 3 further lines as a continuation of the first 3, in 'best' writing.	e.g. 4. Our school is big. 5. It is close to the park. 6. We have won a healthy schools' award.
STEP 3 Total = 15 mins	Totally oral (no writing) VCOP activities: See 'Strategies for Immediate Impact on Writing Standards', 'Write on Track Week 1' and Appendix 2.	
STEP 4 Total = 15 mins 10 mins 5 mins	Sight word activities: Laminated sets of differentiated word cards – 10 to a set, working through from Reception to end of Year 2 lists. Play games. Say and spell words that gave difficulty in Step 2. Identify words with same root/spelling pattern. Reread group paragraph together and praise.	Today is Monday. It is a sunny day. We are all good writers. Our school is big. It is close to the park. We have won a healthy schools' award.

DAY 2

Step 1   (20 mins)

The teacher calls each word in turn, and records it AS the group call out the spelling. Each of the four days begin as follows:

Today is _____(1). It is a _____(2) day.

(1) = name of the day, e.g. Tuesday.
(2) = type of weather, e.g. 'sunny', 'windy', 'cloudy', 'rainy'.

The teacher then leads one further sentence relevant to the pupils, of the type we would call 'news', as on Day 1. The teacher now leads the group in writing the SAME list as was written yesterday. So the model writing may now look something like this:

Today is Tuesday.
It is a wet day.
We go swimming this afternoon.
Our school is big.
It is close to the park.
We have won a healthy schools' award.

 NB The last 3 sentences MUST be identical to the previous day's to enable completion within the time and confidence of pupils.

Read together, and discuss any point that caused difficulty. Each day there should be less.(15 minutes)Pupils asked to copy in best, cursive writing. (5 minutes)

Step 2 (10 minutes)

VCOP activities as on Day 1.

Use same examples but ask pupils to make up more ways of using.

Step 3 (20 minutes)

Up-levelling model writing.

Tell group the writing is at Level 1 because it is in simple sentences only, with no description or higher VCOP.

Ask pupils to discuss in 2s what VCOP they could use to up-level the writing.

Take feedback and model up-levelling by inserting ideas, (Teacher may have to contribute some in the early days) using omission marks, (upside down V) on whiteboard.

E.G.

Today is Tuesday and it is a lovely, sunny day.
Hopefully, we shall all attend swimming this afternoon.
Our school is enormous and is located adjacent to the park.
Amazingly, we have successfully achieved a healthy schools' award.

Reread as a group. Tell them it is now written at Level 4/5.

Step 4 (10 minutes)

Brisk run through same 10 sight words as yesterday, using flash cards. Pupils shout word, spell and shout again. (5 minutes)
Re read the original writing, (omitting the insertions, teacher must model to start) then read the up-levelled model with pupils shouting the up-levelled insertions. Teacher then reads alone with good expression and repeats that it is now Level 4/5.

NB The original writing is still readable, written on widely spread lines, and the up-levelling is through insertion/omission marks (upside down V).

Praise, reward and close lesson.

DAY 2 - OVERVIEW

STEP 1 20 mins	Teacher calls each word in turn, pupils spell and say punctuation. Same opening sentences with detail of day and weather changed. New 3rd sentence, composed by group. Same 3 final sentences. Words that give problems underlined then later copied as a list. Read back. Pupils copy all in 'best' joined writing. Read back.	*e.g.* *Today is Tuesday.* *It is a wet day.* *We go swimming this afternoon.* *Our school is big.* *It is close to the park.* *We have won a healthy schools' award.* **NB** Leave space between each line for up-levelling.
STEP 2 10 mins	VCOP activities as on Day 1. Use same words and punctuation but ask for new examples of ways of using.	
STEP 3 20 mins	Up-levelling model writing. Discuss in 2s / 3s use of VCOP to up-level. Take feedback and agree final decisions. Teacher uses insertion (omission) marks to up-level. Reread twice as a group, including the insertions Teacher tells them it is now Level 4/5.	Today is Tuesday and it is a lovely, sunny day. Hopefully, we shall all attend swimming this afternoon. Our school is enormous and is located adjacent to the park. Amazingly, we have successfully achieved a healthy schools' award.
STEP 4 10 mins	Same 10 sight words as yesterday, using flash cards. Pupils shout word, spell, shout again. Reread original sentences WITHOUT insertions, (teacher models first). Reread up-levelled model, pupils shout insertions. Teacher reads alone with good expression and tells group it is now Level 4/5.	Original is readable because all up-levelling is done above through use of insertion/omission marks. A change of colour for up-levelling also helps.

DAY 3

Step 1   (20 minutes)

The teacher calls each word in turn, and records it AS the group call out the spelling. Each of the four days begin as follows:

Today is _____(1). It is a _____(2) day.

(1) = name of the day, e.g Wednesday..
(2) = type of weather, e.g 'sunny', 'windy', 'cloudy', 'rainy'.

The teacher then leads one further sentence relevant to the pupils, of the type we would call 'news', as on day 1.

The teacher now leads the group in writing the SAME list as was written yesterday. So the model writing may now look something like this:

Today is Wednesday.
It is a windy day.
There is a new bench outside.
Our school is big..
It is close to the park.
We have won a healthy schools' award.

 NB Leave space between each line for up-levelling.

 NB The last 3 sentences. MUST be identical to the previous day's to enable completion within the time and confidence of pupils.

Read together, and discuss any points/spellings that caused difficulty. Each day there should be less. (10 minutes)

Pupils asked to discuss in 2s and remember/identify how it was up-levelled yesterday. Take feedback and use omission marks to insert VCOP.

Pupils asked to copy and up-level in best, cursive handwriting, working in 2s. (10 minutes).

E.G.

Today is Wednesday and it is a wild and windy day.
An amazing, new bench has appeared magically on the field.
Our school is enormous and is located adjacent to the park.
Amazingly, we have successfully achieved a healthy schools' award.

Step 2   (15 minutes)

Sight Word Activities.

Start with Reception word list from NLS and work through to Year 2 over the weeks. Include the key words from the week's writing, so for this first week the words, 'Today', 'is', 'we', 'are', 'going', 'to'.

Use flashcards for pupils to shout the words (5 minutes)

Use sets of laminated flashcards to use in any one of the following ways:

1. Hold up flash cards, pupils call out and spell.

2. Give 2 sets between two, pupils play 'Snap' to win the pairs, saying the words out loud as each is turned over. When a child wins a pair, he/she must say and say and spell the word.

3. Give 2 sets between 3 or 4, pupils shuffle and spread out face down, play turning and matching to win the pairs, saying the word out loud as each is turned over. When a child wins a pair, he/she must say and say and spell the word.

Note carefully record any words pupils are hesitant on spelling. (10 minutes)

Step 3   (10 minutes)

VCOP activities as on Day 1, using the same words as on Day 1.

Step 4   (15minutes)

Embedding spelling:

Use three sight words identified as causing group members greatest difficulty, plus 2 ambitious words from class display. Not more than 5 words in total.

1. Use pointing fingers, (1st finger after thumb) of BOTH hands at once to trace each word, letter by letter, in opposite directions, (i.e. left hand is writing a mirror-image of right hand) large on the table top, saying the letters as they do so. REPEAT. (Pupils may have to do it with each hand consecutively at first.)

2. Close eyes and repeat once. Repeat again if errors.

3. Open eyes. Use pointing finger of left hand to trace word in air above and to left of eyes, looking up at the invisible writing as they do so, (in correct left to right orientation for writing) and saying each letter as they write. TWICE with eyes open then TWICE with eyes shut, but still 'looking up' to left.

4. Open eyes. Write the word on personal white board and show.

> (kinaesthetic/brain based learning methodologies, see Network Press Publications)

Repeat for all 5 words.

Say and spell all 5 words in rapid succession. (10 minutes)

Re-read the original model writing without the insertions. Then read again with the up-levelling. Remind the class it is now Level 4/5

Re-say and spell the 5 words.

Praise, reward and close the lesson.

DAY 3 – OVERVIEW

		E.G.
STEP 1 20 mins	Teacher calls each word in turn, pupils spell and say punctuation. Same opening sentences with detail of day and weather changed. New 3rd sentence, composed by group. Same 3 final sentences. Words that give problems underlined then later copied as a list. Read back. Up-level model writing. Discuss in 2s/3s use of VCOP to up-level, remembering yesterday. Teacher uses insertion (omission) marks to up-level. Reread twice as a group, including the insertions. Teacher tells them it is now Level 4/5. Pupils copy in their best writing	*Today is Wednesday.* *It is a windy day.* *There is a new bench on the field.* *Our school is big.* *It is close to the park.* *We have won a healthy schools' award.* *NB Leave space between each line for up-levelling.* *Today is Wednesday and it is a wild, windy day.* *An amazing, new bench has appeared magically on the field.* *Our school is enormous and is located adjacent to the park.* *Amazingly, we have successfully achieved a healthy schools' award*
STEP 2 15 mins	Sight word activities. Flashcards for 10 target words. Pupils shout, spell, shout. Have sets of cards and play games.	Note any words still causing difficulty.
STEP 3 20 mins	VCOP activities as on Day 1. Use same words and punctuation but ask for new examples of ways of using.	
STEP 4 10 mins	Embedding spelling: Target 3 words causing difficulty plus 2 VCOP words from writing. Use pointing finger to 'write' word large on table top, saying letters out loud. Repeat. Close eyes and repeat. Re-repeat if errors. Open eyes. 'Write' word to upper left in air with pointing finger, spelling out loud. Repeat twice with eyes open, watching, and twice with eyes shut. Open eyes. Write with marker on personal whiteboard and show. All spell together. Reread original sentences WITHOUT insertions (teacher models first). Reread up-levelled model, pupils shout insertions. Teacher reads alone with good expression and tells group it is now Level 4/5.	Original is readable because all up-levelling is done above through use of insertion/omission marks. A change of colour for up-levelling also helps.

DAY 4

Step 1   (5 minutes)

Say and spell the 5 words learnt on Day 3.

Write the 5 words on personal white boards.

Step 2   15 minutes)

VCOP activities as on Day 1. Use same examples but ask pupils to make up more ways of using.

Include an oral up-levelling of a new and simple Level 1 list on the flip chart, working in 2s. Model a Level 4/5 on the board.

E.G.

LEVEL 1 I have a cat.   SCAFFOLD
I have a dog.   And but so also
I do not have a horse.   although sadly

LEVEL 4

Although I have a cat and I also have a dog, sadly I do not have a horse.
(See 'Strategies for Immediate Impact on Writing Standards')

Step 3   (20 minutes)

The teacher calls each word in turn, and records it AS the group call out the spelling. Each of the four days it begins as follows:

Today is _____(1). It is a _____(2) day.

(1) = name of the day, e.g Thursday.
(2) = type of weather, e.g 'sunny', 'windy', 'cloudy', 'rainy'.

The teacher then leads one further sentence relevant to the pupils, of the type we would call 'news', as on Day 1.

The teacher now leads the group in writing the list as was written yesterday.

So the model writing may now look something like this:

Today is Thursday.
It is a rainy day.
Liam's spider has escaped.
Our school is big.
It is close to the park.
We have won a healthy schools' award.

 NB The last 3 sentences MUST be identical to the previous day's to enable completion within the time and confidence of pupils.

Read together (10 minutes)

Pupils asked to discuss in 2s and remember/identify how it was up-levelled yesterday.
Pupils asked to copy in best, cursive writing, up-

levelling as they go. They can work together but BOTH must record as they do.

Teacher uses omission marks to model up-levelling on the main whiteboard.
(10 minutes).

Today is Thursday and it is a wild, windy day.
Catastrophically, Liam's monstrous spider has escaped.
Our school is enormous and is located adjacent to the park.
Amazingly, we have successfully achieved a healthy schools' award.

Step 4   (15 minutes)

Teacher introduces theme for next day's Big Writing.

 NB If Big Writing is on Thursday, this part of the lesson must be interchanged with 'Embedding Spelling', which moves to Friday.

The main class/es will be writing to the fortnightly text focus of the Literacy Unit plan on the second week of each fortnight and will be writing to a different text type previously taught, covering the range over the term, on the interim weeks. (See model on p130)

Whenever possible, the target group should be writing to the same text type as the class, but when this is not appropriate, (because it is an unfamiliar type that they are not meeting because of the intervention) the teacher should select a familiar type to focus on. It should preferably fit to the same title.

The teacher will prepare the group for the text type to be covered and should include at least 3 different activities. The following are some examples:

1. She/he may need to use the OHP to show a similar text type and refresh the characteristics.

2. She/he may use an OHT or Big Book excerpt as a stimulus for discussion.

3. Pupils may brainstorm ideas.

4. Word banks may be built up.

5. Pupils may discuss with a partner.

Pupils use a set of story structure cards each, and an OHT pen to plan (three blue laminated A5 cards, one has OPENING, one BODY, and one ENDING in the middle). Pupils write the 5 key elements; who, what, where, when and how onto each, and underline the one they are going to stop and describe. The class teacher needs to have used the Story Structure cards as a class activity at some point previously. (See Chapter 5.iv, Length, Detail and Description').

If text type is non-narrative sub divide the characteristics of the text type into 3 parts and discuss what may go in each part (all text types can be divided into opening, body and ending for planning purposes).

Take feedback from 2 different pupils each week, starting with most confident.

What ambitious word/s might they use?

> 📌 **NB** To prepare for Big Writing the teacher and class teacher need to agree what text type is this week's focus.
>
> If it is week 2/3 of the NLS Unit plan, the target group will do narrative writing instead of the recommended writing outcome as they have not followed the Unit Plan. The genre should be changed every 2 weeks. On week 1 of each unit the whole class, plus the target group, should be using an alternative text type that everyone is already secure with.
>
> For example:
>
> | 🕐 WEEK | TARGET GROUP -TEXT TYPE | REST OF CLASS – TEXT TYPE |
> |---|---|---|
> | 1 | explanation | explanation |
> | 2 | Science fiction narrative | NLS Unit plan outcome |
> | 3 | report | report |
> | 4 | Historical narrative | NLS Unit plan outcome |
> | 5 | instructions | instructions |
> | 6 | traditional tale | NLS Unit plan outcome |
> | 7 | recount | recount |
> | 8 | report | NLS Unit plan |

Step 5　(5 minutes)

Read up-levelled model writing from Step 2. Praise and remind them that is Level 4.

Say and spell the 5 words studied.

Say an ambitious word they are going to use tomorrow.

Praise, reward and close the lesson.

DAY 4 – OVERVIEW

STEP 1 5 mins	Say and spell 5 words learned on Day 3. Pupils write on personal white boards.	
STEP 2 15 mins	VCOP activities as on Day 1. Use same words and punctuation but ask for new examples of ways of using. Up-level 3 simple sentences using a scaffold. Scaffold e.g.: And but so also although sadly	*Note any words still causing difficulty.* ***E.G.*** *I have a cat.* *I have a dog.* *I do not have a horse.* *BECOMES:* *Although I have a dog and I also have a cat, sadly I do not have a horse. (L4/5)*
STEP 3 20 mins	Teacher calls each word in turn, pupils spell and say punctuation. Same opening sentences with detail of day and weather changed. New 3rd sentence, composed by group. Same 3 final sentences. Words that give problems underlined then later copied as a list. Read back. Up-level model writing. Discuss in 2s/3s use of VCOP to up-level, remembering yesterday. Teacher uses insertion, (omission) marks to up-level. Reread twice as a group, including the insertions. Each pupil copies in 'best' joined writing. Teacher tells them it is now Level 4/5. **NB** Each day pupils are increasingly familiar with process and text and so can achieve more in the time provided.	***E.G.*** *Today is Thursday.* *It is a windy day.* *Liam's spider has escaped.* *Our school is big.* *It is close to the park.* *We have won a healthy schools' award.* *NB Leave space between each line for up-levelling.* *Today is Thursday and it is a wild, windy day.* *Catastrophically, Liam's monstrous spider has escaped.* *Our school is enormous and is located adjacent to the park.* *Amazingly, we have successfully achieved a healthy schools' award.*
STEP 4 15 mins	Planning for Big Writing: Use laminated structure cards –'Opening' 'Body' 'Ending' to record ideas with non-permanent markers. Focus explained in Step 4 of detailed model.	Brainstorm VCOP for Big Writing and record on flip chart. Identify at least 3 of who, what, where, why, how of LDD for each section of structure. Which will be described?
STEP 5 5 mins	Reread up-levelled model from Step 3. Praise and say it is Level 4/5. Say and spell 5 target words. Each pupil names an ambitious word they are going to use tomorrow. Praise.	

BIG WRITING DAY
DAY 5 (May be Thursday or Friday)

The teacher and target group join the rest of the class in the 35 minute oral session before break. They join in all the VCOP activities.

If their intended text type is different from the class's they go to their group room with the target group teacher for the last 10 minutes before break whilst the rest of the class are planning for the NLS Unit plan outcome. They refresh yesterday's planning and extend ideas. They say what ambitious words they are going to use. They receive back their OPENING/BODY/ENDING cards and talk to their friends about the who, what, where, when, how they wrote on.
They decide what description they are going to build into each section.
After break, they work with the teacher in their withdrawal room, so that she/he can provide spellings.

The writing session proceeds exactly as in the classroom including the changes to the environment. The teacher gives the time prompts as for Big Writing:

1. You have had ten minutes. How many different sorts of punctuation have you used? You should use more than 3, make opportunity now.

2. You have had twenty minutes. How many ambitious words have you used? You should use at least three. Can you insert an ambitious adjective or adverb before one of your nouns? Use an omission mark.

.
3. You have had 30 minutes. Look at your sentence openers. Have you opened a sentence with a connective? Have you opened with an 'ly' word? Have you opened with an 'ing' word?

In addition, each pupil has 3 goals, (fruit during the writing session, for example three grapes, segments of tangerine or slices of apple).

When they think they have finished their opening they look at the OPENING card on which they planned their writing (who, what, where, when, how)

Have they written about at least three?
Have they stopped to describe at least one?
Eat a treat and move down a line.

OR (if non-narrative text type)

Look at the 3 part structure of text type in focus:
Have they completed part 1/2/3?
Eat a treat and move down.

Five minutes before the end of the 45 to 50 minute session, the teacher stops the group and asks them to check back to see if they have met their personal target/s. The teacher will have given them these. One child may need to pull the tails, (descenders) below the line. Another may need to check they have a capital letter after every full stop. Another may need to check that 'I' is always a capital and another may need to check that he has used the correct 'their' and 'there'. Most children will have either one or two, (of their three targets) basic skills targets, or one or two, (of their three targets) VCOP targets.

The personal targets will be written in the front of the writing book or folder, so that the teacher can help them check. As they are consistently achieved they are ticked off and a new one added. Gradually they all become VCOP when all basic skills are in place.

The teacher marks the writing. The teacher and class teacher then plan the next week, using a similar range of activities with new examples.

 NB AS THE REPERTOIRE WIDENS, VCOP MUST STILL BE 'RECYCLED' TO REFRESH THE MEMORY, AND ALL SPELLINGS LEARNED SHOULD BE REVISITED HALF TERMLY, OR MORE OFTEN IF ERRORS ARE DETECTED IN ORAL WORK OR WRITING.

Basic skills addressed in this intervention are handwriting, basic sentence structure and punctuation, and spelling. In addition, all pupils should have speaking and listening activities, and should be having one 'fun' lesson a week in Standard English (posh talk). These MUST be taught weekly, usually with the whole class, but consolidated through the intervention. (See Chapter 8, 'The Importance of Basic Skills').

Length, detail and description will also need addressing if they have not already been. The writing structure cards should be on display, (see 'Big Writing – The Method' and Chapter 4, 'What is Effective Target Setting'). However, the teacher may need to build a revisit into use of the structure cards into week 2 or 3 if pupils are still not achieving enough length.

The class teacher should be teaching the current NLS word list, phonics and handwriting in separate lessons that the group are part of.

The following weeks of the intervention, which may be of six to eight weeks, recycle the learning experiences and methodology of Week 1, with the following changes:

1. The 3rd to 6th lines of the writing change each week.

2. The scaffold and simple sentences for up-levelling change each week.

3. The 10 key words drawn from the first three NLS word lists change each week.

4. The 5 focus words (3 of the spellings giving difficulty, plus 2 'VCOP' words) change every week.

5. The order and timings of the steps may change.

6. The range of VCOP focused on will expand, and will probably mirror what is being addressed in the classroom.

7. The VCOP activities will change.

8. The stimulus and text type for Big Writing will change.

Please note: the group should be enjoying the intervention, look forward to attending and be making constant progress in confidence, neatness and accuracy.

LEVEL A   DRAFT

1.	**Can use simple words and phrases to communicate meaning** (majority of work can be read/decoded by an adult without assistance from the child. Must be more than one simple statement).	
2.	**Can produce own ideas for writing.**	
3.	**Can usually give letters a clear shape and orientation** (letters / words can be deciphered even though inaccurate).	
4.	**Can write own name.**	
5.	**Can show some control over word order producing logical statements.**	
6.	**Can make recognisable attempts at spelling words not known** (most decodable without child's help)	
7.	**Can write simple text such as lists, stories, explanations.**	
8.	**Can spell some common monosyllabic words not known** (most decodable without child's help).	
9.	**Begin to show awareness of how full stops are used, in reading or in writing.**	
10.	**Can write with meaning in a series of simple sentences** (may not be correct in punctuation and structure).	
11.	**Can produce short sections of developed ideas** (may be more like spoken than written language).	
12.	**Can use appropriate vocabulary** (should be coherent and mainly sensible).	
13.	**Can use simple phonic strategies when trying to spell unknown words,** (majority is decodable without child's help. If ALL spelling is correct – tick the criteria).	
14.	**Can use ANY connective** (may only ever be 'and') to join 2 simple sentence).	
15.	**Can control use of ascenders/descenders, upper/lower case letters in handwriting, although shape and size may not always be consistent.**	
Total mark		
Level		

Assessment
5/15: (Must achieve criteria 1 – 5) = A1
6 – 10: (First 5 criteria + 1 – 5 others) = A2
11 – 15: (First 5 criteria + 6 – 10 others) = A3/assess for level B

GUIDANCE:
At minimum there should usually be three or more simple statements of three words or more each statement. A simple list of statements all starting with the same key words (e.g. 'I can...' or 'I like...') cannot be assessed above A.1 and the assessor must be clear that the child has selected this strategy for purpose, and that it is not the only list the child is able to produce, i.e. a rote learned strategy.

LEVEL B   DRAFT

1.	**Can communicate ideas and meaning confidently in a series of sentences** (may not be accurate, but mainly 'flows').	
2.	**Can usually sustain narrative /non-narrative** (may not be sustained for B1).	
3.	**Can provide enough detail to interest the reader** (e.g. is beginning to provide additional information or description, beyond a simple list).	
4.	**Can vary sentence openings to interest the reader** (e.g. has a number of ways for opening sentences).	
5.	**Can use interesting and ambitious words sometimes** (should be words not usually used by a child of that age, and not a technical word used in a taught context only, e.g. 'volcano' or 'evaporate').	
6.	**Can match organisation to purpose** (e.g. showing awareness of structure of a letter, openings and endings, importance of reader, organisational devices).	
7.	**Can usually use basic sentence punctuation** (full stops followed by capital letters. May not be accurate for B1).	
8.	**Can use phonetically plausible strategies to spell or attempt to spell unknown polysyllabic word** (if all spelling is correct in a long enough piece to be secure evidence – tick the criteria).	
9.	**Can use connectives other than 'and' to join 2 or more simple sentences** (e.g. but, so, then).	
10.	**Can make writing lively and interesting** (e.g. consciously varies sentence length/uses punctuation to create effect etc.)	
11.	**Can link ideas and events, using strategies to create 'flow'** (e.g. Last time, also, after, then, soon, at last, and another thing...).	
12.	**Can use adjectives and descriptive phrases for detail and emphasis** (consciously selects the adjective for purpose, rather than using a familiar one e.g. – 'the big Billy Goat Gruff').	
13.	**Can spell common monosyllabic words accurately.**	
14.	**Can use accurate and consistent handwriting** (in print at minimum, can use consistent use of upper/lower case, ascenders/descenders, size and form).	
Total mark		
Level		

NB Level B1 may only consist of a few statements (four or more usually). For Level B2 and above, at least one side of A4, or about 100 words or more, is usual.

Assessment:
6 - 8 = B1
9 - 11 = B2
12 - 14 = B3/Assess for Level C

LEVEL C   DRAFT

1.	Can spell common monosyllabic words accurately, and use phonetically plausible strategies to attempt unknown polysyllabic words.	
2.	Can vary sentence structure (from Level B).	
3.	Can produce work which is organised, imaginative and clear (e.g. simple opening and ending).	
4.	Can use a designated form appropriately and consistently (e.g. letters – formal and informal, reporting, diary, dialogue).	
5.	Can adapt chosen form to the audience, (e.g. provide information about character or setting, make a series of points).	
6.	Can use interesting and varied word choices (MUST pick up on 'ambitious' from B5 and can develop use of adjectives and descriptive phrases for detail and emphasis from B12 (consciously selects the adjective for purpose, rather than using a familiar one e.g. – 'the big Billy Goat Gruff')).	
7.	Can develop and extend ideas logically in sequenced sentences (may still be overly detailed or brief).	
8.	Can extend sentences using a wider range of connectives to clarify relationships between points and ideas, (e.g. when, because, if, after, while, also, as well).	
9.	Can usually use correct grammatical structures in sentences (nouns and verbs agree generally).	
10.	Can use sentence punctuation accurately; full stops, capitals and question marks.	
11.	Can structure and organise work clearly including beginning to attempt paragraphs (e.g. beginning, middle, end, letter structure, dialogue structure).	
12.	Can adapt form and style for purpose (e.g. clear difference between formal and informal letters: abbreviated sentences in notes and diaries).	
13.	Is experimenting with a wide range of punctuation, although use may not be accurate (e.g. commas, inverted commas, exclamation marks, apostrophes).	
14.	Can link ideas and events, using strategies to create 'flow' (e.g. Last time, also, after, then, soon, at last, and another thing...).	
15.	Can make writing lively and interesting (e.g. consciously varies sentence length/uses punctuation to create effect etc).	
16.	Can write neatly (although may be slow) (may not be accurate for Level C1).	
Total mark		
Level		

Assessment:
6 - 9 = C1
10– 13 = C2
14 – 16 = C3/Assess for Level D

LEVEL D   DRAFT

1.	Can use, or attempt to use, more than one paragraph.	
2.	Can use correct grammatical structures.	
3.	Can structure and punctuate sentences correctly, (?.,).	
4.	Can use a range of sophisticated connectives (e.g. although, however, never the less).	
5.	Can spell monosyllabic and common polysyllabic words correctly (from Level C)	
6.	Can adapt form and style for purpose (e.g. clear difference between formal and informal letters: abbreviated sentences in notes and diaries).	
7.	Can use adjectives and adverbs for description.	
8.	Can spell phonetically regular, or familiar common polysyllabic words accurately (e.g. 'sometimes', 'bonfire').	
9.	Can develop characters and describe settings, feelings or emotions.	
10.	Can link and relate events, including past, present and future, sensibly (afterwards, before, also, after a while, eventually...).	
11.	Can attempt to give opinion, interest or humour through detail.	
12.	Can use generalising words for style (e.g. sometimes, never, always, often, even, in addition...).	
13.	Can write in a lively and coherent style.	
14.	Can use the designated style confidently.	
15.	Can use interesting language to sustain and develop ideas (MUST pick up on 'ambitious from B5, may be using very adventurous language – sometimes inaccurately).	
16.	Can organise ideas appropriately for both purpose and reader (e.g. captions, headings, fonts, chapters, letter formats, paragraphs, logically sequenced events, contextual and background information etcetera).	
17.	Is beginning to use a wide range of punctuation accurately for effect (. ,( ) ...!? " " -)	
18.	Can write in clear, neat and legible linked handwriting.	
Total mark		
Level		

Assessment:
7– 10= D1
11 – 14 = D2
15– 18 = D3/ Assess for Level E

LEVEL E   DRAFT

1.	Can use a wide range of punctuation accurately for effect (,.?( )!... ''""_)	
2.	Can use ambitious vocabulary (from Level D).	
3.	Can use sophisticated connectives confidently and accurately (e.g. although, however, never the less).	
4.	Can use paragraphs confidently and accurately.	
5.	Can produce thoughtful and considered writing (uses simple explanation, opinion, justification and deduction).	
6.	Can use grammatical structures confidently and attempt grammatically complex structures (e.g. expansion before and after the noun – 'The little, old man who lived on the hill...'; subordinating clauses – 'I felt better when...'; '...who taught me the guitar.').	
7.	Can spell monosyllabic and common polysyllabic words correctly (from Level C)	
8.	Can use nouns, pronouns and tenses accurately and consistently throughout	
9.	Can use a range of adventurous vocabulary for a purpose; some words are particularly well chosen (including adjectives and adverbs for description from D7).	
10.	Can select from a wide range of sophisticated openers and connectives to give order or emphasis (e.g. 'If.....then.....'; 'We.....so as to...').	
11.	Can develop ideas in creative and interesting ways (including can develop characters and describe settings, feelings or emotions from D9).	
12.	Can organise ideas appropriately for both purpose and reader (e.g. captions; headings; fonts, chapters, letter formats, paragraphs, logically sequenced events, contextual and background information etcetera).	
13.	Can spell unfamiliar regular polysyllabic words accurately.	
14.	Can adapt form and style for purpose confidently (e.g. clear difference between formal and informal letters: abbreviated sentences in notes and diaries).	
15.	Can link and relate events, including past, present and future, confidently (afterwards, before, also, after a while, eventually...).	
16.	Can write in a lively and coherent style.	
17.	Can use the designated style confidently.	
18.	Can write in clear, neat and legible linked handwriting.	
Total mark		
Level		

Assessment:
7– 10 = E1
11 – 14= E2
15 – 18 = E3

Writing Assessment: Reception

Criterion Scale Level 1

NAME:

- Can produce own ideas for writing
- Can write own name
- Can show some control over word order producing logical statements
- Can spell some monosyllabic words correctly
- Can make recognisable attempts at spelling words not known (most decodable without the child's help)
- Can write simple text such as lists, stories, explanations
- Begin to show awareness of how full stops are used, in reading or in writing
- Can usually give letters a clear shape and orientation
- Can use simple words and phrases to communicate meaning (9)

 **NB** FINAL NC CRITERIA (9) IS ESSENTIAL TO ATTAIN 1C OR ABOVE

GUIDANCE

At minimum there should usually be three or more simple statements of three words or more each statement. A simple list of statements all starting with the same key words e.g.. 'I can...' or 'I like...' can not be assessed above 1C and the assessor must be clear that the child has selected this strategy for a purpose, and that it is not the only list the child is able to produce, ie, a rote learned strategy

Writing Assessment: Reception

Criterion Scale Level w

The first ten criteria are in the pre-letter formation stage. If the child is making recognizable letter shapes they can be ticked off quickly.

- Will tolerate hand manipulation
- Will work with another to allow mark making using body parts or an implement
- Will attempt to mark make independently
- Can recognise mark making materials
- Can use and enjoys mark making materials
- Can show some control in mark making
- Can produce some recognizable letters
- Can write initial letter of own name
- Will attempt to 'write' things, including own name, using random letters
- Can differentiate between different letters and symbols
- Shows some awareness of sequencing letters
- Will write own name but often with wrong letter formations or mixed upper / lower case
- Can copy over / under a model
- Can imitate adult's writing and understands the purpose of writing
- Is aware of different purposes of writing
- Can ascribe meaning to own mark making ('reads' what has 'written')
- Knows print has meaning and that, in English, is read from left to right and top to bottom
- Can use a pencil and hold it effectively
- Can write own name with appropriate upper and lower case letters
- Can form most letters correctly
- Writes simple regular words
- Begins to make phonic attempts at words
- Writes captions, labels and attempts other simple forms of writing (lists, stories etc)
- Can write single letters or groups of letters which represent meaning
- Can show some control over size, shape, orientation, in writing
- Can say what writing says and means

NAME:

From 'Strategies for Immmediate Impact on Writing Standards' (2003)

Writing Target

NAME:

Connectives	Openers	Punctuation
I can join a sentence using any connective **e.g. 'and'**	I can use simple words to open sentences: **'The...' 'My...' 'I...'**	I can use a few full stops, they may not be in the right place **(.)**
I can use 3 connectives: **'and' 'but' 'so'.** I can sometimes use **'because' 'when'**	I can open sentences with words that show the order things happened: **'First...' 'Then...' 'Last...'** I can open sentences with simple connectives: **'But...' 'So...' 'Then...'**	I can usually use full stops in the right place **(.)** I can always put a capital letter and a full stop **(A .)** I can try to use question marks and commas **(? ,)**
I can use connectives to start sentences **e.g.: 'before' 'after' 'if' 'as well as'**	I can open sentences with harder words to show the order (sequence) things happened: **'Also...' 'After...' 'Soon...' 'Another thing...' 'Because...**	I can always use full stops, capital letters and question marks in the right place **(A . ?)** I can usually use commas and exclamation marks in the right places **(, !)** I can try to use apostrophes in the right places to shorten 2 words (isn't). I can try to use speech marks **("...."）**
I can use harder ways to start and to join sentences **e.g. 'although' ' however'**	I can use harder connectives to open sentences: **'Although...' 'Besides...' 'Even though...' 'Before'**	I can always use commas in the right places for both lists and pauses **(,)** I can always use speech marks in the right places **("_")** I can usually use apostrophes in the right places to shorten and show belonging **(can't)**
I can use a variety of harder ways to start and join sentences e.g. besides' 'even though'	I can use a variety of interesting ways of opening sentences: **e.g. 'After a while...' 'Meanwhile...' 'Before very long...'**	I can try to use other sorts of punctuation **e.g. ellipses (. . .) dash (-) semi-colon (;) colon (:)**

THE 6 QUICK IMPACT LESSON PLANS
ADAPTED FOR YEAR 2
BY THE BRITISH SCHOOL, TOKYO

Lesson 1

Subject: BIG Writing	Year: 2	Teachers: Rebecca, Allison & Karen

Lesson 1	Lesson Focus: Suspense & Monster writing

Objective: to recognise and use descriptive language

Warm-up: Introduce VCOP as 'Very Clever Old Person' and tell children that this is something that they are going to learn about that is going to make them become amazing writers. Write two sentences on board, one with very interesting language and one without. Discuss why one is a better sentence. Say that we are going to be learning lots of 'grown-up' words (vocabulary) and try and use them in speaking and in writing. This is the 'V' in VCOP

Whole Class: Use 'Monsters' excerpts (differentiated). Use highlighters to identify descriptive words. Collect on board.

Pair Activity: Use 'Monsters' excerpts to play 'Find the Word' - working in pairs to find the word or phrase that means the same as the word / phrase that the teacher gives—score goals

Recap what has been said about interesting vocabulary in writing.

Whole Class: OHP: Read 'Howl' and class respond to text. Identify 'WOW' words. Brainstorm more descriptive words for monsters (use the terms adjective & adverb for more able children). Score goals. Discuss likes / dislikes and also suspense.

Independent Writing Activity: Children write next paragraph to continue the story, copying the style of the writing. They use the descriptive word banks to help and focus on using as many 'WOW' words as they can. Stop after ten minutes to ask how many different 'WOW' words children have used so far. Praise. Continue for a further ten minutes and ask again.

Basic Skills check: full stops & capital letters, high frequency words spelt correctly & handwriting!

Plenary: Review learning on vocabulary.

Display 'WOW' words in teaching space as a permanent feature

Resources:	Comments:
VCOP sign OHP & markers 'Howl' excerpt 'Monster' excerpts highlighter pens	

HOWL...

Who would have thought such small creatures could have made so much noise? Bravely, I carried on, clearing a way through all the tiny people as they made their way to the temple.

"Go back!" they said. "Go back before it is too late!" But I carried on into the gloomy night. I had to complete my mission.

Strangely, the inside seemed quiet after the panic of outside. I stood quietly, listening carefully for a sound. All was quiet...too quiet! I waited.

After what seemed like a long time, I crept forward and moved between the chairs and books all over the floor. I didn't make a single sound as I floated towards the tomb at the back of the temple. My hand was resting on the big, cold handle of the door when the crazy, blood-chilling scream ripped through the air. It was the cry of death....

_____

_____

_____

_____

_____

_____

_____

_____

_____

_____

_____

_____

_____

_____

_____

_____

_____

_____

From 'Strategies for Immmediate Impact on Writing Standards' (2003)

Monsters in Stories

The minotaur was a hideous monster, with the body of a man and the head of a cow. It was bloodthirsty and liked eating humans! From deep in the Labyrinth came a terrible bellowing. The ground shook as the mighty monster stamped it's feet.

(Theseus and the Minotaur—Greek myth)

Kailua was a terrible serpent. He had five huge heads with five sets of poisonous teeth. His body was so strong that he could crush you to death. Soon the river was filled with Kaliya's poison. Deadly smoke came up from the water which bubbled and boiled, black and spooky.

(Krishna and the Serpent King—Indian Traditional tale)

The scary monster was green and smelly. Blood dripped out of his mouth as he roared and screamed. His skin was slimy and bumpy with big red blotches. As he came out of his cave, the earth shook.

From 'Strategies for Immmediate Impact on Writing Standards' (2003)

Lesson 2

Subject: BIG Writing	Year: 2	Teachers: Rebecca, Allison & Karen
Lesson 2	Lesson Focus: Snow White in New York	

Objective: to recognise and use a range of connectives.

Warm-up: Recap VCOP as 'Very Clever Old Person' and go over the generic targets. Children think of a range of connectives and teacher records on board. Discuss the use of these words—to show passing of time and structure of events. Choose a connective and children think of sentences using that connective.

Pair Activity: Use connectives cards on tables (differentiated accordingly). Children chose a card and tell their partner a sentence using that connective. Write their best sentence on small whiteboard. Share with class. 'Could we change the sentence by using the connective in a different place?' Discuss the impact on the sentence by using the connective as an opener.

Pair Activity: OHP: 2 excerpts from Snow White in New York. 'Spot the Difference' What makes the second excerpt a higher level than the first? Establish that writing is improved by using a range of interesting connectives.

Short Activity: (Speaking & Listening) 'Spot the Connective' 1 child says a sentence with a connective and the other identifies the connective.

Recap what has been said about using connectives in writing.

Activity: give student story start to Snow White in New York and they highlight connectives.

Independent Writing Activity: Give connective cards to all tables. Children continue the story in the style of the writing using the connective cards to include as many interesting connectives as they can in the writing.
Stop after ten minutes to ask how many different connectives children have used so far. Has anyone used a connective at the beginning of a sentence? Praise. Continue for a further ten minutes and ask again.

Plenary: Review learning on connectives and do oral games.

Display connectives in teaching space as a permanent feature

Resources:	Comments:
connective cards small whiteboards, pens & rubbers 2 excerpts: Snow White in New York highlighter pens	

(extracts from)

Snow White in New York

By Fiona French

Once upon a time in New York there was a poor little rich girl called Snow White. Her mother was dead. For a while she lived happily with her father. Then one day he married again. All the papers said that Snow White's stepmother was the classiest dame in New York. No one knew that she was the Queen of the Underworld. She liked to see herself in the New York Mirror. One day she read something that made her very jealous:

'Snow White—the Belle of New York City'

She plotted to get rid of her stepdaughter

'Take her down town and shoot her,' she said to one of her bodyguards. The man took Snow White deep into the dark streets but he could not do it so he left her there lost and alone. Snow White was about to despair when she heard music coming from an open door so she went inside.

The seven jazz-men were sorry for her and said "Stay here if you like but you'll have to work."

Snow White replied "I'd love to, although what can I do?"

"Can you sing?" they asked.

The first night that Snow White sang there was a newspaper reporter in the club. He knew at once that she would be a

star as well as being very beautiful.

Lesson 3

Subject: BIG Writing	Year: 2	Teachers: Rebecca, Allison & Karen
Lesson 3	Lesson Focus: Katie Morag and the Two Grandmothers	

Objective: to recognise and use a range of openers.

Warm-up: Recap VCOP as 'Very Clever Old Person' and go over the four generic targets. Children think of a range of openers and teacher records on board. Discuss the use of these words—to open the door to a sentence and gain the readers, attention.
Quick-fire examples...who can begin a sentence with...? Which would be the best opener for this sentence...? Who can think of a better opener for this sentence and make it a higher level...?

Whole Class : Use anonymous examples of a child's work to score goals in writing. Pretend it is the work of a recognised writer. Class read together, identify VCOP, especially openers using OHP markers to underline, circle etc. Identify likes and dislikes in the text. Reveal the writer! Praise and score goal!

Recap what has been said about using openers in writing.

Pair Activity: Give children a copy of the letter from Granma Mainland to Katie Morag (based on the QCA Geography unit: An Island Home & the Katie Morag books). Children identify openers by highlighting then work with partner to change to alternative ones.

Independent Writing Activity: Children reply to the letter pretending that they are Katie Morag. They have to explain how she and Grannie Island got Alecina out of the Boggy Loch. Focus on the use of interesting openers. Can they use any connectives as openers? Stop after ten minutes to ask how many different openers children have used so far. Has anyone used a connective at the beginning of a sentence? How many connectives have you used? Praise. Continue for a further ten minutes and ask again.

Basic Skills check: full stops & capital letters, high frequency words spelt correctly & handwriting!
(This will also link to & prepare the children for the QCA DT unit 'Winding Up' where they have to design a pulley system to get Alecina out of the Boggy Loch)
Plenary— Review learning on openers and do oral games.

Display openers in teaching space as a permanent feature

Resources:	openers cards anonymous example of a child's work OHP & markers letter from Granma Mainland letter template from Katie Morag highlighter pens	Comments:

HOWL...

Who would have thought such small creatures could have made so much noise? Bravely, I carried on, clearing a way through all the tiny people as they made their way to the temple.

"Go back!" they said. "Go back before it is too late!" But I carried on into the gloomy night. I had to complete my mission.

Strangely, the inside seemed quiet after the panic of outside. I stood quietly, listening carefully for a sound. All was quiet...too quiet! I waited.

After what seemed like a long time, I crept forward and moved between the chairs and books all over the floor. I didn't make a single sound as I floated towards the tomb at the back of the temple. My hand was resting on the big, cold handle of the door when the crazy, blood-chilling scream ripped through the air. It was the cry of death....

came from the scruffy old tomb...but now there were two tombs! I tried to open one then...a person had been killed! I speedily and quickly shut the old tomb door, but after I shut it, the person who was dead was opening the door. THE PERSON WAS ALIVE!!! I quickly dashed out to the nearest house. I told them all about it.

Ms. G Mainland

Haggis Cottage
Scotland

Dear Katie,

What a disaster! I heard that Grannie Island's sheep, Alecina, got stuck in the Boggy Loch again! How did this happen? I'm sure Grannie Island must be furious with her...the mischievous sheep!

When I spoke to your mother on the telephone, she told me that you helped Grannie Island get Alecina out of the loch. Sadly, she didn't have time to tell me how you managed to do this. Was it difficult? What did you use to help you? Of course, I hope that Alecina was not hurt at all. She really is the most beautiful, elegant sheep on the Isle of Coll.

Write soon Katie, I so look forward to hearing from you. I really would like to know how you and Grannie Island got Alecina out of that muddy, soggy loch.

Lots of Love, Granma Mainland

Grace Mainland

10, Haggis Street
Ulapool
Scotland

Dear Neilly

All my Love, Grace

Lesson 4

Subject: BIG Writing	Year: 2	Teachers: Rebecca, Allison & Karen
Lesson 4	Lesson Focus: Suspense writing	

Objective: to recognise and use a range of punctuation.

Warm-up: Recap VCOP as 'Very Clever Old Person' and go over the generic targets.
Children think of a range of punctuation and teacher records on board, children to come out and illustrate with examples. Introduce Punctuation Pyramid and discuss different levels. Name all punctuation.
Write two sentences on board. Children rewrite at a higher level using the Punctuation Pyramid to help.

Pair Activity: OHP: 2 excerpts from Harry Potter. Study writing and do 'Spot the Difference'. What makes the second piece a higher level? Identify the range of punctuation used in the second piece and try to name all the punctuation.
What else makes the second piece a higher level? Vocabulary? Connectives? Openers?

Recap what has been said about using punctuation in writing.

Activity: OHP: Read text 'The Monster'. Teacher first then together. In pairs, students identify punctuation by highlighting. (**Differentiation:** more able readers to identify all VCOP using a different colour highlighter for each generic target.)
Share likes / dislikes about the passage and talk about suspense. Record 'WOW' words.

Independent Writing Activity: Children write the next paragraph to continue the story, copying the style of the writing. Focus on including a wide range of punctuation.
Stop after ten minutes to ask how many different kinds of punctuation children have used so far. Has anyone used a connective / opener? How many ambitious words have you used? Praise. Continue for a further ten minutes and ask again.
Basic Skills check: full stops & capital letters, high frequency words spelt correctly & handwriting!

Plenary— Review learning on punctuation and do games using punctuation pyramid.

Display punctuation pyramid in teaching space as a permanent feature

Resources:	punctuation pyramid OHP text 'The Monster' 2 excerpts: Harry Potter highlighter pens	Comments:

A man walked down the castle steps. He walked towards the forest as if he did not want to be seen. Harry recognised him. It was Snape. Where was he going?

A hooded figure came swiftly down the front steps of the castle. After reaching the bottom of the mysterious, grey steps, he walked as fast as possible towards the Forbidden Forest. Harry recognised the man's prowling walk...Snape! Craftily sneaking into the forest—what was going on?

From 'Strategies for Immmediate Impact on Writing Standards' (2003)

With fear I padded carefully down the dark, damp tunnel. My hands were shaking so I put them in my pockets. I could see and hear nothing...nothing but the sound of my own panicked breathing. Suddenly an evil smell crept up my nose, like the rotting smell of meat. I stopped, my heart pounding. Was there something in the inky darkness? Before I became even more terrified, I pulled out my torch and shone it up the tunnel. Silence surrounded me but then...out of the blackness came a terrifying shriek..!

Lesson 5

Subject: BIG Writing	Year: 2	Teachers: Rebecca, Allison & Karen
Lesson 5	Lesson Focus: VCOP & scoring goals in writing!	
Objective: to find & use features of good writing		

Warm-up: Who can open a sentence with After / My / choose an opener?
Who can use this connective in a sentence: because / if / before / choose a connective?
Which punctuation would go in/ at the end of this sentence: "Big writing is fantastic!"?
"How many WOW words have I used in my sentence?"
"I can't think of a good opener for this sentence"
"It was all quiet...when Miss O'Connor came in."

Whole Class: Look at Sensational Sentences. Why have I chosen these sentences?
Identify VCOP and give goals to children who wrote the sentences.

Paired Activity: Katie Morag has written a letter to our class but needs some help with her writing. She needs VCOP! Can you help her?

Support – adding VCOP using ^ sign.

Main – writing sentence underneath and adding VCOP

Extension – adding VCOP using target record cards
Independent Activity: After break you are going to write a letter to reply to KM. We are going to practise some sentences that we may use in the letters using VCOP.
What kinds of things are you going to write in your letter?
How is your locality different to her locality?
Answer questions – are you enjoying the books?- do you like painting?
All children have lapboard – travel around 4 bases and write 1 sentence in each.

Base 1: Vocabulary-Write a sentence that includes 1 or more wow words
e.g.. Tokyo is a busy bustling city.
Base 2: Connectives.-Choose a connectives card & use it in a sentence.
e.g.. My locality is different because more people live in Tokyo than on Struay.
Base 3: Openers-Choose an openers card and open a sentence with it.
e.g.. Another thing about living in Tokyo is that there are lots of things to do.
Base 4: Punctuation-Use the pp/punctuation fans to use punctuation in a sentence
e.g.. Do you think you will live on Struay forever?.
Writing Activity: Children use sentences to help write a reply to Katie Morag.

Resources:	sensational sentences support/main/extension letters for editing letter from Katie Morag Letter template for reply	Comments:

Miss Katie Morag McColl

The Shop & Post Office
The Isle of Struay

Dear Year Two Paris,

I am pleased you are reading all my books.

Are you enjoying them.

I like living on the Isle of Struay. I like that my family live here.

It is a really nice island.

Yesterday I went to visit Grannie. She wasn't in.

I went to visit The Lady Artist.

Her paintings are nice.

How do you think Struay is different to or the same as Tokyo.

Love from Katie Morag McColl

Miss Katie Morag McColl

The Shop & Post Office
The Isle of Struay

Dear Year Two Paris,

I am pleased you are reading all my books. (o)

Are you enjoying them. (p)

I like living on the Isle of Struay. I like that my family live here. (c)

It is a really nice island. (v)

Yesterday I went to visit Grannie. She wasn't in. (c)

I went to visit The Lady Artist. (o)

Her paintings are nice. (v)

How do you think Struay is different to or the same as Tokyo. (p)

Love from Katie Morag McColl

Dear Katie

Love from

Sensational Sentences!!

1. Grannie Island is very cross with Alecina but she has been exasperating these days.

2. First we got a ladder but it didn't work.

3. Meanwhile, when you were at the show, we were at the Post Office.

4. Before very long we had Alecina out of the Boggy Loch.

5. I will tell you all about Grannie's glittering, beautiful sheep.

6. It worked!

Lesson 6

Subject: BIG Writing	Year: 2	Teachers: Rebecca, Allison & Karen
Lesson 6	Lesson Focus: VCOP	

Objective: to find & use features of good writing

Warm-up: Use punctuation fans to show punctuation that should be used in the following written sentences: "Katie Morag couldn't believe it...Alecina was stuck in the Boggy Loch!"
                    "Who, do you think, lives in Hermit's Hut?"
Children say their own sentences & identify punctuation they would use.

Group Activity: Letter from Neilly Beag to Granma Mainland (enlarge to A3). 4 groups work together to identify & highlight VCOP

Group 1	Vocabulary
Group 2	Connectives
Group 3	Openers
Group 4	Punctuation

Paired Activity: Give simple sentences on whiteboard & pairs work to level-up writing using VCOP—write new sentences on lapboards. Pairs then work on a PS for the letter.

Independent Activity: write a reply from Granma Mainland to Neilly Beag.
VCOP check after 10 minutes. (this is a lead up to Katie Morag & the Wedding, next week's Geography when Neilly & Granma Mainland get married!)

Resources: punctuation fans
             letter from Neilly Beag
             reply template for letter from Granma Mainland
             highlighter pens
             lapboards, pens & rubbers
	Comments:

Neilly P. Beg

2nd house in The Village
The Isle of Struay
Scotland

Dear Grace

First, I would like to say how much I enjoyed your visit to the island this weekend. Although the weather was stormy, I still had a fascinating time with you and so enjoyed our suppers by the fire! Actually...I think you are totally amazing! Even though it is a lot to ask, I would like you to visit our beautiful island again next weekend because I have something incredibly important to ask you. After you have decided if you can come, could you send me a letter to let me know?

All my Love, Neilly

Grace Mainland

10, Haggis Street
Ulapool
Scotland

Dear Neilly

All my Love, Grace

Michelle Wraith, Big Writing Consultant
Lorraine Bell, Big Writing Consultant
Agnes McGrogan, Big Writing Consultant

Headteacher, staff and pupils of Linthwaite Clough JIN School, Kirklees
Headteacher, staff and pupils of Heaton Primary School, Bradford
Headteacher, staff and pupils of Gainsborough Primary School, London
Headteacher, staff and pupils of All Saints' Primary School, Isle of Wight
Headteacher, staff and pupils of Graveney Primary School, Kent
Headteacher, staff and pupils of Rotherhithe Primary School, London
Headteacher, staff and pupils of New Hall JINC School, Sutton Coldfield
Headteacher, staff and pupils of Wilsden Primary School, Bingley
Headteacher, staff and pupils of Glebe Junior School, Derbyshire
Headteacher, staff and pupils of Usher Street Primary School, Bradford
Headteacher, staff and pupils of Love Lane Primary School, Isle of Wight
Headteacher, staff and pupils of Crossley Hall Primary School, Bradford
Headteacher, staff and pupils of British School Tokyo

Gail Newton, Linthwaite Clough JIN School, Kirklees
The Assessment Group, West Dunbarton, Scotland
Ian McCollum, 'All Write Now', Derbyshire
Jane Troth, Graveney Primary School, Kent
Steve Jessop, Bishopspark, Germany
Anna Burt, Poplar Partnership Action Zone
Janet Mort, Derbyshire
Steph. Naylor, Yorkshire
Zoe Mawson, Heaton Primary School, Bradford (Assistant Headteacher)
Sallie Boulter, All Saints' Primary School, Isle of Wight
Jasmine Dower, Rotherhithe Primary School, London
Anna Jaremko and Heather Hudson, New Hall JINC School, Sutton Coldfield
Maria Blakely, Wilsden Primary School, Bingley
Rebecca Harris and Nonie Adams, British School Tokyo
Sue Beckett, Christ Church CE Primary School
Steve Bartlett, Love Lane First School, Isle of Wight
Julia Horsington, Southern Road Primary School, Leeds
Kay Priestley, Pudsey Waterloo Primary School, Leeds
Maureen Janane, Education Bradford
Carol Satterthwaite, Education Bradford
Dorrie Brown, Farnham Primary School, Bradford
Gill Holland, Education Bradford
Michael Thorpe, Swain House Primary School, Bradford

The many talented teachers, Senior Managers and LEA Officers across the country who
have raised standards so successfully through implementing 'The Big Write' in schools.